The
Quick and Easy Way
to
Take Control
Of
Your Life

The Quick and Easy Way to Take Control of Your Life

What the internet won't tell you about goal setting

Author
Dr. Emma Frost
2016

Printed in the United States of America

First Printing, 2016 ISBN 978-0-9940519-2-9

CanLead Publishing, Winnipeg, Manitoba, Canada.
www.canlead.ca

www.ruleyourworld.ca

For Lucy Hughes

Because one day she will rule the world.

CONTENTS

FOREWORD

Don't read this book if you like being stuck.

Goal setting, while not complicated, is incredibly hard to do successfully. In fact, it's no wonder why less than 10% of people follow their New Year's resolutions.

You might have picked up this book to help you with your work, your health, your relationship, or even cleaning your garage. Well I have news for you. Just like that coffee table from IKEA, you need to follow the instructions if want to guarantee success.

What Dr. Frost has created is your instruction manual. Now you need to follow it.

With every business I built I had goals - same for every mountain I climbed or race I entered. And, no question, those goals propelled me further and took me to great heights. What I didn't do was employ the power and secret of goals in the rest of my life. Somehow I assumed goals didn't work for money, relationships, or even gratitude. But they do. In fact, we are hard-wired to follow goals.

The trick is to create the goals properly, follow them faithfully and to not discard them when you stray.

Once you develop your goal setting, goal keeping habit a small miracle begins to unfold... you become a promise-keeper. And promise-keepers have the resolve and capacity to take on any challenge or goal they think they are worthy of and is important enough.

As Zig Ziglar once said "What you get by achieving your goals is not as important as what you become by achieving your goals."

Now it's time to get started to develop your goal setting, goal keeping habit.

Hugh Culver

Author, speaker, CEO getSOS.net

ACKNOWLEDGMENTS

There are always people to thank. To my friends (in no particular order) Nina, Max, Pat, Ann, Robyn, Seajay, Kate, Sly, Emma, Jan, Carole, and Dawn, who provided suggestions, feedback, and rude remarks to help me be better. Thanks to Michael for inspiring me to write this. I owe a debt of gratitude to all the people I have met that have provided me with the stories I have used to illustrate my ideas. Thanks to Spike for reminding me when it is time for tea. Thanks to Mrs. McPherson at the car dealership, for making me set a deadline to finish! Finally, and most importantly thanks to Kathi for being supportive, motivational and my best friend in all the right ways.

INTRODUCTION

Everyone bumps into something that makes them stop and think at some point in their life. They may shrug it off and carry on, or they might realize they need to make changes. In 2012, I bumped into another car, head-on at 30kph. I walked away with just a few scratches and bruises to show for it.

Although I was not physically affected, I was mentally shattered. I realized that I had to do some serious thinking about my life and where I was going. Over the next few months, I realized I had to make some significant changes in my life. I walked away from my career to follow my passion for helping people take control of their

> *"If you don't like how things are, change it! You're not a tree."*
> Jim Rohn

lives. Ironically, I was only just taking control of my own life.

There were many changes I had to make. I had to plan. When I started to plan, I found that I had to set goals so that I had something to plan for. I had never set goals before, and it was a new experience for me. I started searching the internet for help and quickly found that there is a lot of advice out there, but nothing that taught me what I wanted to know. I made many mistakes with my goals, some of which set me back. Others that led me astray. Several times, I found myself wandering way off track. It wasn't until I analyzed the process of goal setting that I found out where I was going wrong. In the last few years, I have provided guidance and training to many people looking to make changes in their lives. The number one skill that they lack is how to set quality goals. Hence, I sat down to write this book.

For many people, the only time they set goals is on December 31st. The tradition of  New Year's goal setting began over 2600 years ago in the Babylonian era. There are no records telling us about the success rate of the ancient populations of Babylonia and Rome, but by the end of the 1930's about 25% of Americans were making New Year's resolutions. Currently, about 45% of Americans make resolutions, but only 8% achieve them. Most people forget their goals within a week.

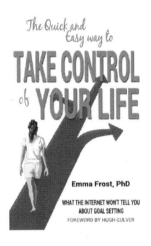

The Quick and Easy way to **TAKE CONTROL of YOUR LIFE**

Emma Frost, PhD

WHAT THE INTERNET WON'T TELL YOU ABOUT GOAL SETTING
FOREWORD BY HUGH CULVER

There are many reasons to set goals besides New Year's tradition. The number one reason is so that you can **take control of your life**. They also increase focus and enthusiasm.

Additionally, goals help you make progress towards being the fabulous person you know you are. When we dream about what we want, we get excited and hopeful for the future. We can see a way to change our lives. By setting goals, we can make short-term and long-term changes. When I set my goals, I gained in confidence, knowing that I was more likely to succeed. As you develop new skills and increase your knowledge, your self-esteem grows.

As you have bought this book, I expect you want to take control of your life. The first step you need to take is to dream a little and decide what you want out of life. Then you need to write down those ideas and turn them into workable goals.

You can spend weeks searching the internet for help on goal setting, there are (literally) millions of web pages with ideas, suggestions and helpful comments to guide you. Unless you pay big bucks, there are no actual classes available. This book is designed as a guide *and* a workbook. As you read through you will find exercises to complete, so that by the end of the book you will have at least one, well-crafted goal and a plan for success. There is also a lot of space for notes and ideas. Once you have created one goal, you can go on and create more. As many as you like. As big as you wish. The bigger they are, the more exciting they get.

I was brought up by bibliophiles, and the idea of writing in a book appalls me. If you are the same, or run out of space in the book, you can go online and download extra worksheets. You will find them at www.ruleyourworld.ca

On the web page, you will find more information on personal development, and a discussion forum for readers of this book. Because it is so important to have support when you start to change your life, the discussion forum will give you a place to share your fears, receive encouragement, and make new friends. You might even be inspired to grow your dreams into goals and become utterly fabulous!

Emma Frost

Part I

Goal Setting 101

WHY SHOULD I SET GOALS?

A s children, we dream of the future, we fantasize about being utterly fabulous. We don't let the reality of life get in the way of our imagination. Then we find that we are not entirely in charge of our lives, and we lose sight of our

> "We cannot become what we need to be by remaining what we are."
> Max de Pree

early dreams. We learn the rules of society, accepting that parents, teachers, bosses, and spouses must influence our lives. For many people, those early dreams are lost in the mists of time, and we forget that we should be in control of our lives. We lose sight of our fabulousness.

Your fabulous never goes away, you just need to find where it is hiding, and release it.

21

Many people are not even aware that they are unhappy with their lives, and are not mindful of the fact that they can take back control. I have dedicated my life to helping people find their fabulous, take back control of their lives, and be the person they knew they could be before life got in the way.

Goals help you take charge. They provide a target for you to aim at. They give you a purpose, and provide opportunities for growth and development. Some people have a to-do-list for the day or week ahead. This can be an excellent way to ensure that you get everything done that you need to get done. However, very few people have a list of things that they want to achieve over the next year, five years, or over their lifetime. They may have, at some point, thought about running a marathon, or going to Disneyland, or traveling around Europe for six months. Without creating a way for that to happen, their wishes become dreams, and dreams rarely come true. Without realizing it, they have lost control of their lives.

By setting goals, you can plan how to get out of your rut and take back control of your life. In my early 30's I realized that I had become stuck in a rut. I hadn't realized how dark and gloomy my life had become. I had been walking the same path for so long that my particular furrow was now deeper than I was tall. Because I had not developed a plan to change the direction of my life, I had no way to get out of that rut. Just making the decision to take control of my life made everything brighter and I was able to hope that my life could change. I believe that because I felt better about my future, I became a better prospect for employers, and was finally offered a job after eight years of trying. People sometimes find themselves in exactly this same situation, but don't know how to take back control.

> "If you are in a rut and want to get out of it, you need to find a way to climb the walls, no matter how high they have become."
> Emma Frost, Ph.D

If you are in a rut and want to get out, you need to find a way to climb the walls, no matter how high they have become. You just need to get your foot on the first step of that ladder. Goals can help you get there. Goals can make a difference. You need to construct your goals carefully, and that is the purpose of this book.

As you work through the exercises in each section, your dream will become an attainable goal. I frequently use climbing Everest as an analogy for creating huge goals. As I was  researching for this book, I found a website that describes how to get to the top of the world. As I read the page, I suddenly realized that if I wanted to climb Everest, I could! It was a revelation to me. Not because I want to climb Everest, but because I realized that if I wanted to, I too could stand on the top of the world, just by planning carefully. I looked at my personal goals, and then made them bigger and more fabulous. Because I realized that I could. In addition, I realized that I *am* worth the extra big outcomes, I *am* allowed to drive a really nice car, and live in a beautiful house.

I *am* allowed to be me.

I want to achieve my goals because I am excited about the end points. This is an important feature of goal setting. It is important to know specifics about your goal, to know what your target will be. For example, if you decide to lose weight, you don't just say, *"I want to lose weight."* You specify how much weight you wish to lose, and in how much time. *"I want to lose ten pounds before I go to Cancun in March."* The same applies to all of your targets. To run faster or further, to earn more money, or to improve your education. Without a target, it's hard to know where to begin, let alone where you will end!

> *"If you really want to do something, you will find a way. If you don't, you will find an excuse."*
> Jim Rohn

***

This book will guide you through the process. You can develop an achievable goal, plan to succeed, and track your progress all in one place.

Types of Goal

There are essentially five types of goal:

1. **Immediate:** Twenty-four hours to one week

   These are quick goals, can be part of your to-do-list. Things you want to achieve today and this week. Immediate goals can also be part of a longer-term goal.

2. **Short-term:** Eight days to three months

   These goals need more time, and probably more thought. They are what you want to achieve in the next few weeks to 3 months. Again, short-term goals can be part of a bigger goal

3. **Intermediate-term:** Three to twelve months

   These are things you want to achieve by the end of the year. You can also accomplish intermediate goals by completing immediate and short-term goals.

4. **Long-term:** One to five years

   What you want to achieve in the next few years. Most businesses use a 5-year plan to ensure continuity of growth.

Some people start to think about retiring five years before they plan to stop work. You can design a one to five-year plan to help you get to a life changing goal.

5. **Lifetime:** Five years and beyond

As the name suggests, this is a plan for an ultimate goal. To climb Everest, to make a billion dollars, to win an Oscar. These are all lifetime goals. They are often made up of many short-term, intermediate and long-term goals, require a well-described plan of action, and may include multiple people (family, work, etc.).

When you start to come up with ideas for your goals, you can then put them into the different types. Rather than thinking about things you want to achieve in a day, week, month or year. Think about what you want to accomplish, and then decide how much time you need. I set a goal of owning a new car. For some people, that could be a short-term goal. For others, it might be an intermediate target. For me, it is a long-term goal. I will need more than one year to save up

27

the money to buy a new car. If your goal is to earn a degree in fine arts, you need to allow four years to achieve this. If your goal is to learn to paint with watercolors, you might be looking at an intermediate or even short-term goal.

It is easier to identify your goal first and then decide which type it is. Remember that it is also ok to have several long-term or lifetime goals, without having immediate or short-term goals. Because they are your personal goals, you are the one who decides how much time you need to ensure success.

Exercise 1

Take some time to think about what you want to achieve. It is best if you don't rush this part.

This book is designed to help you make a change in your life. If you need to walk away from the book and think, that is ok. If you need to sleep on it, that is ok too. Whatever you need to do, you do.

You can also come back to this exercise later as inspiration hits when you complete a few more exercises.

Make a list of your dreams:

_____

_____

_____

_____

_____

_____

_____

_____

Categorize your goals using the following table. It doesn't matter if you don't fill up all the categories. It is more important that you start thinking about your goals. If you have more than one idea per category, that is ok too. The boxes contain examples to help you.

Immediate	Remember to pick up milk on the way home
Short-term	Save up $500 so that I can buy concert tickets to see Beyonce in August
Intermediate	Lose 10 pounds before I see my mother at Christmas
Long-term	Get a new job, with higher pay and better benefits before Summer next year
Lifetime	Retire by the time I am 50

~ Emma Frost ~

IN WHICH ASPECT OF MY LIFE SHOULD I SET GOALS?

Y̲ou can set goals in any area of your life where you want to see change. When I first ventured out into the world of employment, I had no direction, and, as a result, drifted from job to job. I worked at a hair salon, a fish store, and a bar. I had no ambition and no commitment to my future, and no goals (I just didn't realize it back then). When I landed a full-time job, my new boss asked me where I wanted to be in five years' time. I realized that I had never thought of my future or my expectations. Because of that conversation, I understood that the job I had taken was for only two years. I didn't want to be looking for a new job every two years. I wanted one that I could rely on for regular income for the rest of my life. So I was forced to plan for my future.

Before settling on developing a career, I decided that I wanted a job that I could have for more than two years. That was a long-term goal, and I realized that to achieve this aim, I would have to become a better employee. I worked 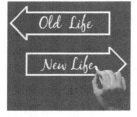 hard at learning the new skills required for my position, and at getting to work on time! Short-term goals that meant I had a greater chance of succeeding in my long-term objective. Although, at the time I still wasn't aware that I was setting goals!

It is not compulsory to set a lifetime goal. Some people just can't think that far ahead. Especially if you have settled into a rut and are having a hard time seeing a way out of it. Once you start to set smaller, immediate and short-term goals, you will see changes in your life that will help you think about big, long-term and lifetime goals.

Another hurdle you may have to overcome is that of the control of another person, or of your situation. A friend of mine (Karen) had always secretly wanted to travel. Deep in her heart, she longed to lie on a beach all day reading a book. Karen never told anyone about her dream because she couldn't imagine how it could ever come true. She was in a bad marriage and had no income.

One Saturday, Karen went to the movie "Shirley Valentine" with a friend. She was inspired by how Shirley changed her drab and dreary life and lived her dream. Karen's biggest challenge was talking to her husband. The most interesting aspect of this story was that when she finally plucked up the courage to tell him she wanted to live life and not watch it go by, he told her that he had been trying to work out how to say that he wanted out too. They went through an amicable divorce and parted ways.

I met Karen just after she got her first job as a server at a steak house. She was so excited

35

because finally, she could save up to take that vacation that she had dreamed about. Once she took control of her life, her imagination took flight. Karen was able to overcome the obstacles because achieving her goal became more important than the status quo of her life.

You can set goals for work, family, community, self-development, financial and physical (health) aspects of your life. When you first start out, it is not important to have a goal in each of these categories. You might want to start small with a goal of spending more time with your family, or a physical goal of losing some weight. It doesn't matter where you begin; it just matters that you *start*.

There are six categories of goal:

1. Health
2. Self-development
3. Family
4. Financial
5. Work
6. Community

1. Health

I am a great believer in putting self first. This is critical because your health is the most important thing for you to look after. If you don't, no one else will. If you always put others first, then the rest of your life will fail. I have heard people say their family is their number one concern, but if they don't look after their self, they won't be able to take care of their family. I know a lady

> "Nourishing yourself in a way that helps you blossom in the direction you want to go is attainable, and you are worth the effort."
> Deborah Day

who, a few years ago, was close to death. Jane had put her health and wellbeing to one side and focused all her energy on her two sons (both in their late twenties, one married with a baby).

One day I met her at the hospital where I was working, and spent some time chatting with her. Jane hadn't told her sons that she was ill because she didn't want them to know. It was more important to her that they come first. They relied on her for so much (according to her). She did their laundry, bought their groceries, and was never reimbursed. Jane confessed to me that recently she had gone without to provide them with what they needed, and was several months behind on her rent.

I convinced Jane to tell her sons that she was sick and needed help. When she finally spoke up, they were so mad at her for not telling them sooner. The oldest son immediately arranged for her to move in with his family and wouldn't accept any money from her. He also paid off her debts to the property owner and utility company. The youngest son stopped taking his laundry to her, and admitted that he had a machine in his apartment building, but couldn't be bothered to use it. Neither son had realized how much Jane had sacrificed for them, as she had never said. Now that she was ill, they were both prepared to take care of her. Jane recovered after about 18 months and still lives with her oldest son. Nevertheless, she is so much happier and relaxed. Her whole life has changed, because for once she put herself first.

2. Self-Development

Self-development is second on the list. You should always be looking to learn and grow. It doesn't matter how you do that. You can read, take classes (in person or online), attend public lectures at the local university, or take up a new hobby. Self-development is all about improving your awareness of the world around you; developing your own personality; maximise your potential, and increase your enjoyment of life. I have a friend, Robert, who is just completing his Fine Arts undergraduate degree, he is in his 70's. He is thinking of doing a Philosophy degree next. He is choosing subjects that interest him, that are expanding his world.

You can join special interest groups or take part in community activities. I had a very dear friend who was a strong believer in life-long learning. Les had a long and successful working life. When he retired in his 60's, he decided to continue with his personal growth, and he joined a local Toastmasters Club[1]. I met him

---

[1] Toastmasters International is a volunteer organization dedicated to training leaders and speakers around the world. Find out more at www.toastmasters.org

almost 20 years later, and his only regret in life was that he hadn't joined Toastmasters when he was young. You can work on your personal growth many ways. Whatever you chose to do, make sure you are having fun.

3. Family

Your family life is an important area to develop goals. Again, this is part of knowing where you are going in life. Family is one of the categories where you need to work with other people to develop goals. You can have your own family based goals, such as get married, have three children, etc. but you know that once another person is involved there needs to be compromise to ensure everything works out.

Family is also an area where your plans may need to change according to external forces over which you have no control. I had a friend several years ago, who wanted nothing more than to get married and settle down. She planned her wedding. She bought wedding dress patterns. She subscribed to wedding related magazines. She never met Mr. Right, or even Mr. Hewilldo. She is still single in her late 50's and has accepted that she will probably remain that way. She just never had the opportunity to achieve that particular goal. Then again, my mother remarried aged 62, and I have read about people marrying in their 80's and 90's, so never say never!

Family-based goals define what you want for each other, and allow you to plan to succeed as a team. Because every family is different, there really are no guidelines on setting family goals. People usually focus on shared activities, such as holidays, shared ideals, such as volunteering for a local organization, or shared dreams, such as the kind of house you want to live in. They may also set goals to sit down to dinner as a family once a week, or go out together one night a week.

> *"I have always argued that change becomes stressful and overwhelming only when you've lost any sense of the constancy of your life. You need firm ground to stand on. From there, you can deal with that change."*
> Richard Nelson Bolles

41

Goals can bring you closer together as a family, and will enrich your life. Working as a team may also mean that you can think bigger because there are more people to work on achieving your goals. It is certain that family-based goals will make you all stronger and more successful.

4. Financial

Financial goals are an excellent way to stay in control of your life. Money is a source of worry for most people. It is one of the top reasons why relationships end. It is also the number one source of stress for adults. By setting financial goals, you will also be able to achieve much more. Sometimes the money is part of another goal, such as a vacation, or new car. Sometimes it is part of a long-term goal, such as to retire aged 50. Whatever your financial goals are, it is important that everyone in your immediate family be on the same page and working together.

5. Work

At some point in everyone's life, we have to work to make money. By setting work-related goals, we increase our chances of success. For most people, that means a regular promotion and associated increase in income. Very early in my work life, I realized that I needed to think about where I wanted my life to go. I had drifted into a job that I could do without too much effort and talked about wanting something more. I complained for many years but did nothing. It was only when I finally realized that I actually had to act rather than just talk, that I was able to set the right goals. Once I knew what I needed to do, I was able to set goals and make steps towards achieving them. As I reached consecutive goals, I was finally able to make the changes that I had been talking about for so long.

Work focused goals may be something simple such as *"get to work on time every day"* or *"learn a new job-related skill."* You may also plan for longer-term changes such as *"get more qualifications"* or *"get trained for a new career."* My friend Ken had been in retail for over 30 years of his life when he was made redundant. He decided that he needed a change of career and started training to be a health care aide. It was the perfect job for him, and he is now very popular at the nursing home where he works. He changed his career at the age of 54. When I walked away from my research career after 32 years, I didn't have to decide whether it was the right thing to do or not. It was something I had to do. I wasn't thinking about leaving a career as much as I was thinking about following my passion for helping others. It doesn't matter what your motivation is; the point is that you take that step and make that change.

6. Community

The community is on this list because participating in activities in the community can open up your life to an entirely new world of opportunity. There are many benefits to interacting with your neighbors and joining in local events. There are many ways to be part of society. You can influence your environment by joining local groups, or you can shape the world by joining international groups.

You can buy many books about how to make a difference in your life. "The Eco-Optimist's Guide to Saving Our Planet" by Deanna Ford (available Fall 2016), provides hundreds of ideas on how to get involved. It isn't essential that you have a set of aims in this category. They may come later as you start to see different aspects of your life change. Community goals can include volunteering, or participating in local events. Benefits include the phenomenon known as "*helper's high*." This is the feeling of happiness

> "In as little as 10 minutes, you can help heal our planet! My book is jam-packed with doable ideas to fit any interest, budget and schedule"
> Deanna Ford

and well-being that you get from helping someone without requiring a reward. One activity that I try to get involved in each year is the local community clean up. Even if I can't make it out on the day of the official litter pick-up, I will remove litter from the street as I walk along. No one will ever thank me for doing that, but it makes me feel good to make a small difference in the appearance of my neighborhood.

You have already written down some ideas. Use these as a starting point for Exercise 2. The order of goal categories is crucial to ensure that you have (and maintain) balance in your life.

Exercise 2

Using your thoughts from Exercise 1, sort them into categories using the table below. It is important to note that the groups are listed in this order for a reason.

Personal Health	
Self-development	
Family	
Financial	
Work	
Community	

How to Create Goals

Now that you have decided to start making goals, you need to think about what you want to achieve. If your goal is to spend more time with your family, choose how much time and if there is a particular day for that (i.e., Sunday all day). If you aim to lose weight, decide how much and how long you will give yourself to do it.

When I decided to make some goals, I had trouble thinking of things. Here are a few suggestions to get you going.

1. Buy a new car
2. Write a book
3. Finish my degree
4. Save up for a once in a lifetime vacation down under

5. Rewrite my resume and apply for 100 jobs
6. Learn to play the guitar
7. See the Superbowl live
8. Be in a play
9. Sell one of my paintings
10. Go parachuting

There are more suggestions on the website www.ruleyourworld.ca

Once you have set one goal, you will begin to find other targets to aim at. I recently sat down to write my list of goals for this year. I decided to add buying a new car to the list. Once I thought about that and realized my perfect car is a Caddy, other ideas rushed into my head. I have a list of five goals that I will be striving to achieve this year. I will let you know how I do, so check out my Goal Setting page at www.ruleyourworld.ca

By using your heart as well as your head when you are creating your goals, you will be connected to your goal. If you only set goals that *need* to be done, life will get very boring very

50

quickly. Being attached to your goal is vital to increase your chance of success. In addition, by using your heart, you will be setting goals that you *want* to achieve, like my lipstick red Caddy.

It is important to note that sometimes goals are very selfish things. In the pursuit of your goal, you may have to inconvenience other people. For example, if your goal is to run a marathon, you will have to spend many hours training, running and working out. If your partner has no interest in running, you will need to have their full support to prevent resentment building up in the relationship. It is also entirely possible that in the pursuit of your goals, you change many things in your life, and find that you no longer share a common path with the people in your life.

Several years ago, I was sharing an apartment with a friend, and we had been roommates for over a year. I had moved away from home to get some peace and quiet and to have some control over my life. As the year passed, I realized that I still didn't have control over my life. There was always someone else there, someone making noise, eating all the food and using up all the shampoo.

I was not doing some things because it would have been too disruptive to her and I didn't want to concede any more. I realized that I needed to get a place on my own. Our lease was due for renewal, and I started to look for somewhere else to live. I didn't discuss this with my roommate before making the decision because I was afraid of her reaction. I didn't like confrontation and knew that she would be upset. I also knew that if I told her I was looking at other places to live, she would want to come too and that I wouldn't say no. It was very stressful, sneaking around behind her back to inspect places, taking phone calls from property

> "The most powerful relationship you will ever have is the relationship with yourself."
> Steve Maraboli

owners and agents in private. I convinced myself that it would all work out in the end.

It all came to a head when she mentioned looking for a new place to live, and I had to confess that I had already signed the lease on a nice little studio apartment two streets away. Because I knew I wasn't strong enough to stand up to her and say no, this is what I want, and I don't care what you want. I didn't give her enough time to find a new place. She had to move back home. She was very upset with me, and we didn't speak for a long time after that. Nonetheless, it was what I had to do to achieve my personal goal. I needed the freedom to grow and change. It was one of the hardest things I had ever done, but I knew that it was a turning point in my life.

Looking back at that time in my life, I realize that I lacked confidence and wasn't able to stand up for what I wanted out of life. That was the first time I put myself first. Even so, it was many years before I finally took control of my life.

By putting others ahead of yourself, you are less likely to achieve your goals. Of course, you have to be considerate of others. You can encourage them to join you in achieving the aim, or help them set their own goals. If they don't want to, don't let that stop you, but you may have to modify your journey. Make it a long-term goal rather than an intermediate one to give the other person time to come to terms with the changes you are making in your life. Or perhaps, modify your life like I had to.

You may have to compromise on some things to succeed. You may go against the wishes of another person in your pursuit of change. Only you can decide whether to continue or change your goal to accommodate others. There are also times when you will need to be selfish to achieve your aim. When I made the decision to strike out on my own and live alone, I had to upset some people to succeed. This happened to me when I sought

> "Overcome your barriers, intend the best, and be patient. You will enjoy more balance, more growth, more income, and more fun!"
> Jack Canfield

to continue with my education, which ultimately took me to America.

When I left the UK, I left behind my family and friends, several of whom thought I would return to the UK within six months. What many people didn't know was that my move was one step in a bigger life goal, if I had gone back, I wouldn't have achieved that goal. Only one of my friends understood that and supported me through the dramatic changes that I had to make. Sometimes you may need to reassess the situation you are in and take back control of your life so that you can grow and move forward.

Personal growth may take longer than you expect. It is like growing bamboo. You work hard on the bamboo, you feed and nurture it, and you see no growth. You put more effort into it, add more plant food, and move it to a sunnier spot. You think you see a little growth. So for three years you keep feeding it, watering it, and caring for it. Just when you are about to give up on your bamboo shoot, it grows three feet overnight.

The changes that you make in your life may take time, as long as you stick with it, you will succeed.

Wording Your Goal

Once you have decided what you want to change, think about wording your goal using dynamic language (do, will, can, etc.), try to avoid negative terms (don't, won't, can't, etc.). By keeping your goals active and positive, they become more attractive to you. If you can only think of a negative way to phrase something like *"Don't eat chips for lunch."* Try changing it to *"Eat healthy meals."* The most important thing to remember though is that this is *your* goal. Word the goal the way that works for you. If you start to feel that you are doing something wrong, remember there *is* no wrong way, that different doesn't mean wrong and there are many right ways to do things. These are also useful mantras (see more on p.87) when you start to feel self-doubt and fear.

Another tip to increase your chances of success is by using the present tense. If you use future tense, *"I will... I shall..."* you are not expressing a willingness to complete the task in reality, not just in your imagination. Instead, use the present tense *"I am..."* When I quit smoking (for the fifth time), I told myself *"I am not a smoker."* This was an excellent way to remind myself that I really didn't want to smoke again. In this way, you are telling yourself that this is something that you are working on now. It becomes immediate; it is in the now. You can also use *"going to..."* which indicates a plan or prediction. This will make your goal more tangible. *"I am going to lose 30 pounds before December 31st."* It feels more real than *"I would like to..."*

Exercise 3

Pick one of the ideas that you have come up with in the previous exercises and turn it into a positive, active statement.

_____

_____

_____

_____

_____

59

What is Your Motivation?

When you are writing your goals, include a sentence or two explaining *why* you want to meet this objective. It will help with your motivation when you find walls in your path further along the journey. With the weight loss goal, your reason may be so that you can wear your bikini on the beach without embarrassment, or so you don't need to buy a completely new wardrobe. By reminding yourself of your reasons, you are more likely to stay on track and succeed.

You will also realize why you have chosen that goal. If you are anything like me, you decide to lose weight and are all gangbusters for the first few weeks. Then you hit the plateau and lose all the impetus. If I decided to lose weight to increase my self-confidence, I would be struggling very quickly as I inevitably put the weight back on, plus some. Once you have pinned down your reason, you can revise your goal accordingly. I met Jason a few years ago who told me that as a child, he had always wanted to be a dentist. He was an accountant and had forgotten about wanting to be a dentist until I had specifically asked him to remember his childhood dreams. When I asked him why he had wanted to spend his life poking around in people's mouths, his response was surprising. His childhood dentist had driven a flashy car and being a young boy this impressed him and influenced his career choice. I asked if he was driving a flashy car now and he shook his head. I explained to him that his goal was the car, not the career, and nothing was stopping him from getting a flashy car now. A few months later I met Jason again, and he was driving a little blue convertible. Jason told me that when he went to buy the car, he was more excited than he had been in years. And that driving around in his flashy car he felt like he was on top of the world. Jason had finally achieved his childhood goal. One that he had forgotten about in the process of living.

> "What lies behind us and what lies before us are tiny matters compared to what lies within us."
> Ralph Waldo Emerson

Exercise 4

What is the reason behind your goal?

_____

_____

_____

_____

_____

_____

WRITE YOUR GOALS DOWN

You have already started to do this. And if you have put this book down for any length of time, you are already aware of the most important reason to write your goals down! *To help you remember them.* Imagine if you hadn't written anything down. Would you be able to remember your ideas and thoughts?

By writing down your goals, not only are you validating your intentions, but you are also creating a stronger memory of that intention. As a result, you will be more aware of your goal, and it is more likely to play a role in guiding your future activities. It also significantly increases your chances of success.

The most common reason people set goals is the New Year. However, an extensive study (4.5

million respondents) showed that 91% of people fail with their New Years' Resolutions. There are various reasons for this massively high failure rate, including forgetting about the goals (23%), not keeping track of progress (33%) and being unrealistic (35%). Also, ten percent of the respondents said that they had set too many resolutions and were overwhelmed, which is almost guaranteed to end in failure. Other studies of goal setting

> "By recording your dreams and goals on paper, you set in motion the process of becoming the person you most want to be."
> Mark Victor Hansen

success strategies have shown that even if you are 100% confident of success, you are still 52% likely to fail. Men succeed more than women do, and females fare better when supported in their goals by their friends.

A Harvard business school study in 1979 found that eighty four percent of their graduate students had no goals, thirteen percent had goals but had not written them down, and three percent had written goals and plans to succeed. Ten years later, the researchers re-interviewed the class and found that the 84% of students with no goals were earning, on average, half the salary received by the 13% who had unwritten goals. The three percent who *had* written down their aims were making, *ten times as much* as the other ninety seven percent added together. All of these studies provide strong evidence that writing down and planning your goals, significantly increases your chances of success.

The act of writing down the words will also connect you to the goal more closely. You have turned it from an abstract thought to a real concept. By writing it down, you are stating your intention, and validating that intention. It also helps you to refine the goal so that it is easy to understand.

In addition to writing your goals down, find a picture to represent your goal and put it somewhere you will see often. Stick it into the back of this book or on the wall by your bed. It doesn't matter where, only that you see it often. This will keep you motivated. Seeing the picture is a reminder that your goal is tangible and not just imaginary. I have an image of a lovely red

Caddy pinned to the wall over my desk. Every time I look at it, I am re-motivated to reach my goal.

Be aware that familiarity breeds contempt, and after a while, you will no longer see the picture or the words that you  have written. They will just be there. To prevent this and maintain motivation, you will need to move the images and words around the house. Get new pictures, and post your goals in a different place. Write your affirmations on the mirror.

Do what you need to do to stay in control!

Exercise 5

Write down one of your goals devised in the first three exercises, without going back to see what you had already written. i.e. from memory.

_____

_____

_____

_____

Were you able to easily remember your ideas?

Find a picture to represent your end point, and stick it in here.

KEEP THE NUMBER DOWN

Numerous studies have shown that you can only keep five to seven things in your short-term (working) memory at any one time. By trying to keep more than seven items on the go, you lose focus and are less likely to complete a task. With five goals or fewer, you are much more likely to remember the goals that you have set for yourself.

As you are looking to set goals in more than one area of your life, you can have a *total* of more than five goals. The more categories of goal you have, the fewer you should have in each category. Don't forget that you can turn some of your goals into the steps needed to reach a bigger goal.

You could have two primary goals: a life goal and a work goal. You can set these objectives as long-term goals, and then add two to three smaller goals under each of the bigger aims.

Remember that you can add new targets when you complete previous ones. You can also revise your goals. I will talk about that more in later chapters.

If you have already come up with eight goals, don't delete them. You can prioritize, and put off the ones that can wait until you have completed others. I will talk about prioritizing in a later chapter (p.195).

Exercise 6

If you have identified two ideas that can be classified as big goals, write them down. If not, look back at your goals and see if any of them are potentially major goals. Then insert them here.

Don't forget to include your reasons!

1. _____

_____

_____

2. _____

_____

Beware of Assumptions

Assumptions are factors that you assume or believe to be true without any proof. They are usually based on experience. We assume that the coffee we buy at the drive-through is what we order. We assume that the bus will come at or around the time it says on the schedule. We assume that the weatherman will be semi-accurate. We have to assume some things because otherwise, life would be rough. However, assumptions can hold you back. If we assume we will never win the lottery, we would never buy a ticket.

One dangerous assumption that we make is that our parents are right about everything, and if they tell you that you can't do something, you assume you can't. I had a friend who wanted to learn to ride a motorbike, but her father had told her that she couldn't. He told her that she wasn't strong enough to hold the bike upright, and not coordinated enough to drive the machine. She assumed that he was correct until one day another friend offered to let her ride his bike in the parking lot. He went behind her just in case, but she found that not only was she strong enough to hold the bike upright, that she was more than capable of driving the motorcycle. She had shied away from motorbikes based on the assumption that her father was correct.

Assumptions can be positive as well as negative. Positive assumptions are those that give us confidence. If we assume that we can pass exams, we go into the room with more confidence and are more likely to pass. If we assume we can do something, we will try. When I was fourteen, I decided to do some baking. I browsed through my mother's recipe books and selected a recipe for brandy snaps. I followed the recipe and made a plate full of cookies. When my mother came home, she couldn't believe that I had made them. She said, *"you shouldn't be able to make those. They are really complicated!"* Well, I didn't know that I wasn't supposed to be able to make them, and it didn't occur to me that the recipe was complicated. Therefore, I succeeded where I might not have tried if I had listened to my mother's assumptions before I started baking. Incidentally, I have never made them since!

The brain is a fascinating structure because it is designed to ensure the greatest chance of our survival. As such, unexpected or unusual situations increase our fear so that we are prepared in the event we need to fight to survive, or run away. Fear is one of the most dominant effectors of our actions. As you can see from the figure below, more of the brain is activated by fear than by happiness. Other emotions such as fear, joy, and excitement can also significantly influence our memory of experiences. When

Happiness   Fear

77

we encounter a new situation, our brain runs through our previous experiences to work out how to react.

Because bad experiences are more firmly embedded and closely tied to our emotions, they are the first things we remember. As a result, we sometimes find ourselves shying away from repeating an experience, just in case things go wrong again.

When I first learned to drive, aged 17, I nearly killed the instructor and myself. It was several years before I tried to drive

> *"Don't build roadblocks out of assumptions."*
> Lorii Myers

again because I assumed that I was a terrible driver. I wasn't, but my self-confidence was shattered. Self-assumptions may also be based on words that have been used by people who influence you such as parents, siblings or teachers. These frequently take the form of self-doubts. When you are thinking about your assumptions, reflect on where they came from.

Often people are not aware of the assumptions they are making. When I was 14, I joined a field hockey club. My phys. ed. teacher had recommended that I become a member. I was shy and quiet, didn't have the right gear, and was using a stick that was so ancient it was shaped like the letter L. I played for that Club for 15 years growing as an individual and as a player. I purchased new sticks and equipment. I trained hard, and I was one of the most reliable players on the team. Yet many of the Club members still thought of me as a 14-year-old the whole time.

This wouldn't have mattered, except that I wasn't considered mature enough to be on the Club committee or play on the first team. I was 21 when this first came up, and I was so frustrated that they assumed I hadn't grown up and changed in seven years. They

> "Begin challenging your own assumptions. Your assumptions are your windows on the world. Scrub them off every once in while, or the light won't come in."
> Alan Alda

finally, grudgingly, allowed me to play on the first team, but only because there wasn't another goalie. However, the other team members felt they had to coach me, and didn't include me in strategy discussions. Because I was shy and not pushy, many people assumed I had nothing to contribute. However, at that time, I was coaching a county junior team and had my own strategies, which I was happy to share if they asked me. I think the most upsetting part of their assumptions was that I was also deemed irresponsible and blamed for losing equipment that I had never been given.

It is important to understand how assumptions may drive your thinking. Also, how they can cause problems if they are incorrect. It isn't always easy to identify your assumptions because we often believe them to be truths. Through the identification of the source of the assumptions, you can start to change them. You can start to train yourself not to believe them.

Some assumptions that people make include:

- I don't deserve to be successful.
- Everyone is watching me and waiting for me to fail.
- I don't deserve to be happy.
- Someone else will do this better than I can.
- That is too difficult for me to do.

80

- This is too hard and not worth the effort.
- This will take less time than they say.
- This is easy.
- I know all about that.
- If I ignore it, it will go away.
- I have plenty of time.

When you are developing your goals and plans, examine your expectations of each step. Ask yourself if you are assuming anything. If you are, check to see if the assumption is based on fact. If it turns out to be wrong, you can adjust your plans accordingly. When I first thought about starting my own business, I was worried that I couldn't succeed. This was based on my own assumption that I am financially incompetent and likely to go bankrupt. I thought long and hard because I really wanted to make a difference in people's lives by helping them take back control. I looked into business courses and discovered that there were many avenues of help. I took many classes, on all aspects of business and I now have my own company. I am not afraid to ask lots of

> "When you're surrounded by people who share the same set of assumptions as you, you start to think that's reality."
> Emily Levine

questions and ask for help. I have received a tremendous amount of support from many people. You may need to set your ego aside and ask for help when you need it. It is ok to not know everything.

As long as you believe in yourself, you will find people who are willing to help, especially people who have had the same experiences.

Exercise 7

Write down your assumptions

_____

_____

_____

_____

_____

Assumptions can be self-defeating and are one of the most common hurdles that people have to overcome on their way to greatness. Luckily, there are ways to address them.

If you find yourself thinking, "*I couldn't possibly...*" or "*What am I thinking?*" Then stop yourself and think. Are you getting in your own way? Pin down the assumption and work out where it came from. Then ask yourself if it is true. If you don't know, then ask yourself why you believe the words.

> "One day you will realize that you can be everything you want. It just takes planning, timing, heart, passion and the courage to risk it all. Stand up and be proud of your fabulousness."
> Emma Frost, Ph.D.

Many years ago, I was in a terrible place. Nothing was going right. There was no one to support or encourage me, and I was close to giving up on everything. I was full of self-doubt fueled by many people telling me that I was making huge mistakes, that I should just accept my limitations and stay buried in the deep rut that was my life. There was only one thing stopping me, a tiny little voice deep down inside me that said: *"you do deserve this, you can do it, you can succeed."*

I am a great believer in affirmations. I have used them many times over the years. Back then, I wrote down several positive statements on a sheet of paper, put them in a frame, and hung them in the bathroom. Every morning, as I bathed, I read the statements out loud. It was tough at first, for two main reasons: 1) I was scared to believe them, and 2) I was *really* scared to believe them. As the days and weeks went by I found it easier to speak the words, and more importantly, I began to feel them. My sheet of affirmations got me through the last twelve months of my Ph.D.

What can you use as affirmations? Anything that will help you get past your stumbling block. One I suggest to everyone is **"I am allowed to be me."** A statement that is powerful and emotional, and oh so effective. Other phrases can include "*I am worth it*" or "*I can do this.*" Whatever you decide to use must be personalized to you. Everyone has their self-doubts, and negative thoughts about themselves. Some know people who work to undermine their confidence. Don't let those doubts stop you from achieving your goals.

Other examples of affirmations are:

- I have done nothing wrong
- There is no wrong way
- Different is good
- I am strong
- Every day, in every way, I'm getting better and better[2]
- I am fit, healthy and attractive
- I forgive those who have harmed me in my past and peacefully detach from them
- I possess the qualities needed to be hugely successful
- I trust myself
- I am a good person

Affirmations can also help you complete tasks that you really dislike. When I was doing my Ph.D., one of my tasks was to count red blobs down a microscope. I hated it with a passion and put off counting until I couldn't put it off any longer. Then I was faced with hours and hours of counting. I forced myself to sit at the microscope and count saying, *"I really enjoy counting red blobs, I am having a really*

---

[2] Attributable to Émile Coué de la Châtaigneraie

good time doing this, I am more than happy to spend hours sitting here counting blobs." The more I said the words, the less I hated the task. The less that I hated the work, the easier it became to sit down and complete the task. Yes, it took me hours, but it wasn't the hateful task that my negativity had turned it into.

When developing affirmations, you can also take the negative assumptions that you have identified and reverse them. Thus, *"I am not good enough"* becomes *"I AM good enough"* *"I can't manage"* becomes *"I CAN manage."* Remember that these phrases can change as you grow and develop. They can also change as you move forward with your goals.

> *"By affirming your own gifts and accomplishments, you build your confidence and increase your ability to build a brighter future."*
> Debbie Ford

Exercise 8

Write your affirmations here:

_____

_____

_____

_____

_____

Print this page up and pin it to your wall. Look
at it every day, and say the words out loud.

~ Emma Frost ~

Part II

Creating Your Goals

MAKE YOUR GOALS "SMART"

There are many ways to go about setting your goals. If you have taken a course or read a web page or a book about goal setting (including this one), you have probably heard of SMART goal setting. If you are like me, you are probably resistant to being told what to do, or how to do things. I like to develop my own way using experience, knowledge, and research, but in this instance SMART really is the best model to use, even though it has been done to death on the internet.

SMART is an acronym that provides criteria to guide you as you set your goals. The words are used as guides as you develop your goals. It can be an acronym for many different things, pick the words that work best for you. The essence of the SMART criteria is what is important.

S – Specific/Significant/Strategic/Suitable

M – Measurable/Meaningful

A – Achievable/Actionable/Ambitious
/Audacious

R – Realistic/Reasonable/Results-based
/Relevant

T – Timely/Time-bound/Time limited

Some sources add E and R to the acronym.

E – Exciting/Educational/Evaluated

R – Recorded/Rewarding/Re-evaluated
/Re-assessed

Your goal needs to be well written to give yourself the greatest chance of success. By following the SMART criteria, you are building increased potential for success. In this chapter, I will discuss the component words of the acronym, and how they will add value to your goal. Consider each component word as you read and decide which you will apply to your goal and only use those that increase your chances of success. You can go back and change your goals as you work through the book. Don't be afraid to throw out a goal and start again from scratch. Do what you need to do to be comfortable with your choices.

Choose one of the ideas that you developed in the first exercises to work on.

_____

_____

_____

_____

_____

S

Specific/ Simple/ Strategic/ Suitable

1. Specific

A **specific** goal is focused and detailed. When you reread the goal several months after making it, you should immediately know exactly what needs to be done to be successful.

> *Poor:* To learn a foreign language.
>
> *Better:* Learn Spanish so that I can communicate with the waiters when I go to Mexico in October

Be precise. Use clear and unambiguous language. What do you want to accomplish? Who is involved? When must it be completed? Why do you wish to achieve this goal?

97

There should be no confusion about your intention. By starting your goal statement with the word "I" and making it in the present tense you are making the goal real. Now add the specifics. "I am playing with my children every day and reading them a bed time story every evening by Dec 2016"; "I am sitting behind the steering wheel and proudly driving my brand new lipstick red Cadillac ATS by Dec 30, 2016." Whatever your goal is, when you read it you see yourself achieve it.

2. Simple

Simple is always better, no matter what you are doing. By keeping your goal simple, you are increasing the chances of success.

If you have more than one action in your aim, split it in two and prioritize to ensure success. For example, if you want to earn more money so that you can buy a bigger house, by splitting that goal in two, you stand a better chance of succeeding. Now your *"Increase my earnings by $5000 this year and buy a house."* Becomes *"Increase my earnings by $5000 this year,"* and *"Buy a house this year."* The simplified goals are now less daunting, and you will increase your satisfaction level by two! Also, it is easy to prioritize because you need to earn more money to buy the new house.

3. Significant

You may have heard people say that the journey to the destination is an experience on its own. This is true for goal setting too. You may need to make a change in your lifestyle, attitude, beliefs or character to be successful. The person you become from

> *"The major reason for setting a goal is for what it makes of you to accomplish it. What it makes of you will always be the far greater value than what you get."*
> Jim Rohn

achieving a **significant** goal is someone who is more likely to achieve success in the future. I am a Toastmaster. I joined in 2002 and quickly earned my first certificate. The last time I had won a certificate was 20 years ago and decided I wanted to get more. Therefore, I set myself a goal to obtain my advanced award. This was a *significant* goal for me, and I grew so much in the following two years as I worked on developing my skills.

4. Strategic

A **strategic** objective is not the same as a strategy. A strategy is a plan. You develop a strategy to achieve a specific task. A goal is a step in the plan. A strategic goal is a well-planned and thought out objective. It may have short-term and intermediate aims built in.

Your goal should be more than just an end-point. There needs to be a process built in. A process is basically a consecutive series of stages or steps that get you to the result you are aiming for. For example, if your goal is to decorate your house, there is a process, a series of steps you need to take. First, you need to choose a new color scheme, and then you need to buy the paint and any other equipment that you might need (brushes, cleaner, drop cloths).

Before you start painting, you need to move (or cover) the furniture and tape around areas that you don't want to paint (light switches, etc.). There are many other steps involved, but you get the point. These steps need to be in some sort of order so that you increase your chances of success. For example, you wouldn't buy paint before choosing your new colour scheme. Other steps can be completed in any order, for instance, you might clean up before you remove the tape from the windows.

As you work towards your goal, the steps you take to make changes ultimately change you, as my Toastmaster's goals did for me. You may need to learn a new skill, or improve your knowledge of something. You may need to break or develop habits. These changes will stay with you long after you have achieved your objective.

Succeed

Change

Grow

Learn

If your goal is to find a new job, you will have to make some changes in your life to succeed. You may need to retrain, or learn new skills. You will also need to create a great resume. In the process of working towards a new job, you will learn about yourself and may generate more ideas for longer term goals. No matter what, if even if you don't get the new job your life will be much better because there is always a reason behind searching for a new job.

Of course, when you do eventually get a new job, your stress levels will go down, your income may go up, you may find yourself with more spare time. This will benefit you in many ways, including increasing your self-esteem. When you add a learning component to your goal, you open up all kinds of new possibilities. When I joined the Toastmasters club back in 2002, I had no idea where it would take me. The communication and leadership skills that I have developed and the things that I have learned have driven me in an entirely different direction than I had ever considered. I own a business. I am a motivational speaker, author, and success coach. All because I decided to improve my communication skills.

> "We are each gifted in a unique and important way. It is our privilege and our adventure to discover our own special light."
> Evelyn Mary Dunbar

The personal growth opportunities I took helped me to get to where I am now. If I had never stepped into that room to find out about the club, I wouldn't be where I am now. You never know where your new found skills will take you. In addition, the friends that I have made along the way are like family to me now. My life has been enhanced in ways I could never have anticipated.

5. Suitable

You need to ensure that the aims you are working on are still **suitable** for your success. They also need to be appropriate for *you*, as you change, as your world changes. When I was a child, I wanted to be a dancer. I wanted to be on stage in front of a large crowd, getting a standing ovation from the audience. My mother signed me up for ballet lessons. I started classes when I was six years old. I enjoyed the dancing, learning the steps, and moving to the music. I had danced for five years before I discovered that I had stage fright. I was ok if I was at the back of the chorus, but not if I had to be in the spotlight. I kept taking ballet lessons wondering if, one day, I would be able to be the prima ballerina.

As I grew, I got too big to be a professional dancer (as one of the "nicer" dancers pointed out to me one day). I also realized that I didn't like the nylon tights or thin soled shoes, nor did I like having my hair scraped back into a painful bun. When I realized that I didn't really enjoy ballet, I quit dancing. I never lost the goal of being in the spotlight, but I did tuck it away into a corner of my being, along with all the other dreams I didn't share with others. I tried acting but found that stage fright kept me out of the spotlight. It was only recently that I realized public speaking is my way to the limelight. I identified my goal through a process that was more appropriate for me. I now have to plan to achieve this aim.

Making sure your goals are suitable will also keep you from being unrealistic. You might want to run a marathon in June, but that goal may not be appropriate for your body type, health, and current fitness level if you make the goal in March. You also need to make sure that your process is appropriate for the goal. If your goal is to get fit, you won't sign up for a marathon in June if the only running you do now is to catch a bus. If your goal is to write a best-selling murder mystery, you wouldn't just sit down at your computer and start writing without plotting the story first.

You may also need to break habits to succeed. For most people, changing their habits is one of the hardest things to do, but one of the most important. When I quit smoking, the most difficult part

> "A change in bad habits leads to a change in life."
> Jenny Craig

was overcoming the cravings I felt when I drank coffee because I always smoked when I had coffee!

If in doubt about your process, think about everything that might go wrong at each step. If one of the steps is unattainable, you need to revise the process. Remember, you can't plan for every eventuality. If you have a plan B for every step, you may spend all your time planning and never actually get to step one!

Exercise 9

Does your goal meet the **S** factor?

If not, how can you make it more specific, simple and/or suitable?

Rework your goal:

_____

_____

_____

_____

Don't spend too much time on this stage of the process, you may find your goal becomes more S-word (specific, simple and/or suitable) as you proceed through the next steps.

Measurable/Meaningful

1. Measurable.

Being able to **measure** your goal is important for many reasons. The first one being that you need to know when you have achieved success. If your goal is to get fit, how will you know when you have reached your goal without specifying how fit you want to get? If your goal is to improve your education, you need to decide what you mean by improvement or specify the certificate/diploma or degree you want to achieve. The other part of having a measurable goal is knowing where you started out. If your goal is to lose ten pounds, but you don't know how much you weighed when you

109

started dieting/exercising, how will you know when you have reached your goal? Don't forget to write down your starting point, even if you think you will remember; you might not.

Part of making your goal measurable is deciding upon a method of quantification. For example, continuing your education might mean gaining certification in a career-related subject. Or it might mean getting a fine arts degree just for fun. When you are setting down on paper how you will quantify your goal and the progress you are making, it is important 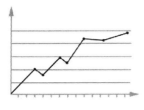 that you stick to one method of measuring. If you decided to lose ten pounds but weighed yourself on a different set of scales each time, you would never know when you actually lost ten pounds. In the same way, if your goal is to run a mile without stopping and you don't measure how far you run, how will you know that you have run a mile?

As well as knowing when you have achieved your goal, by measuring your progress as you go along you will be able to assess your development. It will keep you motivated to continue as you see steady progress towards the goal. Especially when you are trying to lose

> *Poor:* To read more books this year.
>
> *Better:* To read forty books this year

weight, which can be quite a struggle. When you lose a pound, and then another, you will be motivated to stick to your weight loss regime. If you enroll in a diploma program, by keeping track of your grades and exam scores you will be able to see yourself completing the course and achieving the new designation.

When working on your goal, ask yourself the following the questions:

- How much?
- How many?
- How far?
- How big?

Don't forget that part of being able to measure your goal is knowing where you started. Write down your starting point in your plan. It doesn't need to be part of the goal itself.

2. Meaningful.

A **meaningful** goal is something that you will be proud to achieve, something that excites you. A meaningful goal may also change your life. Either as you progress through the steps, or when you have completed the goal. When I decided to improve my education, I set my goal high and decided that I wanted to get a Ph.D. When I achieved my goal, it was incredibly meaningful to me. It caused a dramatic change in my career and personal life because I moved to the US. More than that, by achieving my goal I felt empowered and finally in control of my own life. When I set those goals for myself, I used my heart as well as my head. By using my heart, I became emotionally invested in the outcome. Achieving the goal became more important to me and was very satisfying to complete successfully. When you are setting your goal, consider how you will feel when you achieve it.

- Will you feel proud?
- Will you feel satisfied?
- Will you feel independent?
- Will you feel empowered?

These are all important factors to take into account because they are part of making your goal meaningful.

Exercise 10

How will you measure your progress?

Where are you starting from?

Have you described your quantification process in the goal?

Write down your measurable goal:

_____

_____

_____

_____

How will you feel when you have completed your goal?

_____

Achievable/Actionable/ Ambitious/Audacious

1. Achievable.

The only reason to set goals is so that you can grow and develop. If you set goals that are *easily* achieved, there is no challenge. However, you also have to be careful to set goals that you do stand some chance of reaching. A goal should feel attainable so you won't give up. One way to stay motivated is to remind yourself why you set the goal.

Another part of making your goal **achievable** is by not expecting too much too soon. When I was (much) younger, I set a goal of running a half-marathon. I had six months to

117

train and was already
reasonably fit. I was
disappointed that I
wasn't able to run for
two hours without
stopping the first time I
went out to run. I was

Poor: Win an Oscar for best director!

Better: Direct a play at the local theatre group this year.

used to running all out for up to four or five minutes at a time, depending on which sport I was playing, but I was not an endurance runner. I had to learn to pace myself.

By realizing that my progress would not be rapid, over time I was able to learn to pace myself, and successfully completed the run. The friends I had run with then decided to tackle a full marathon, but I knew that I would never be able to finish a 26-mile run. I encouraged them, supported them, and turned out to cheer them on the day, but for me, that goal was unachievable.

2. Actionable

When writing your goals, include an **action** verb, such as stop, start, end, read, etc. Try to avoid passive or negative words (e.g. don't, can't, etc.). It is much easier to do something than not to do something. I once had the goal "don't eat between meals." I lasted about three days because I found myself resenting the goal, it was telling me what I *couldn't* do. Make sure that when you read your goal, you know how you are going to achieve success. For example, if you need to find a new dentist, setting yourself the goal of "find a new dentist" is not a well-written goal. By adding action to the goal, "phone Delilah and ask her which dentist she uses" lets you know how you will complete the task.

In this way, you can also make sure that your goal can be completed. Many years ago, I  set myself a goal of making a lot of money. That was my goal, "make a lot of money." Without any form of action written in. Needless to say, I have still not achieved that goal.

Another way to improve your chances of success is to word your intent in the present tense. By including yourself in the wording, you also increase your likelihood of success. This is because when you read the goals they become affirmations (or mantras) and become more firmly embedded in your brain. Instead of, "make a lot of money" I should have written down "I am making a lot of money." This process links into the process of convincing yourself that you are worthy of succeeding with your goal. As well as helping you to visualize your life the way you want it to be.

When you phrase your goal, write it so that every reader knows how you will achieve success.

3. Ambitious

When you think about your goal, ask yourself if you will be stretching yourself to attain it. Try to be **ambitious** and think of something that will test you. The phrase "think outside the box" is often used to describe activities that don't fall into "normal behavior." Think about an interest that you would like to participate in, or perhaps improve on. By challenging yourself this way, you will learn new things about yourself. As you realise what you can do, you will be able to stretch yourself further with goals that are more ambitious.

One way to make your goal ambitious is to "add some." For example, if you want to read more books next year, think about how many you read now. Do you read one a week? One a month? Then base your number on that. Then add 10%. This will stretch you and will require more thought and planning. When I decided to run a half marathon, I was being ambitious because I had never run that far, or for that long.

How To Become Creative

For some people, coming up with something new or different is not an easy task. If you search the internet for help on developing your creativity, you will find a myriad of sites, most of which don't help. The best way to come up with new ideas is to take a shower. There is no documented evidence, but it is well known in the neuroscience field, that when you stop thinking your brain can make random connections. In this way, ideas will pop into your head, memories will come to the fore, and your creativity is allowed free reign.

> "Creativity involves breaking out of established patterns in order to look at things in a different way."
> Edward de Bono

For this same reason, we often come up with fantastic ideas just as we fall asleep. Creativity is something that we can develop with a little effort. One idea is to take an everyday object, such as a paper clip and come up with ten or more different uses for the item. If you take a different thing each day and think up different ways to use the item, with time you will find it easier and easier to come up with different ideas. You can devise lists of things too, book titles that you want to write, ways to improve air travel, or titles for country and western songs. I once spent an hour coming up with excuses to give my boss for being an hour late for work. In this way, you will be opening up your creativity, letting your brain link random thoughts and ideas together.

The basis of creativity is using your imagination to connect ideas that were not previously linked. It doesn't matter what you come up with. The important thing is to start to think more extensively, beyond your normal limits. As you begin to get used to coming up with ten things, increase the number to fifteen. Keep stretching yourself. Set yourself a time limit, so you don't spend all day coming up with new uses for last year's birthday cards, and you will soon find yourself thinking more and more creatively!

> "Creativity can be described as letting go of certainties. "
> Gail Sheehy

It is great to think big. It is well known that the more ambitious your goal, the greater the reward. However, if you are overly ambitious when setting your goals, you may become discouraged if you don't see progress. I recently set myself a weight loss goal. For my height, I am supposed to weigh 145 lbs. I haven't weighed 145 lbs since I was 21 and training to run that half marathon. If I set my goal as 145 lbs, I wouldn't even bother to diet because I know I will never be able to sustain that weight in the long term. I have set my goal weight, and it is an ambitious goal, but it is realistic. I just have to stay committed to that goal. If you are determined, have the ability to achieve it, and there is no reason why you shouldn't succeed, you are guaranteed to triumph.

4. Audacious

That doesn't mean that you can't be **audacious**! Choose something that will surprise yourself, and others. Be bold, daring, courageous and confident! Show the world how utterly fabulous you are! The bigger the goal, the more excited you will get. The more exciting the goal, the more you will be motivated to

> *"So the reality is that you just have to say, 'I'm more committed to my vision than I'm committed to your doubt or my fear,' and just go for it..."*
> Jack Canfield

succeed. The excitement of possibility drives us to take action. Regardless of whether we ever reach the target, allowing ourselves to dream big enriches our lives.

I am working on a current, audacious goal of speaking in front of a sell-out crowd of 5000 people. Does that goal scare me? Yes, it does. However, it also excites me, and that is why I will continue to pursue my dream.

~ Emma Frost ~

Exercise 11

Have you described your action in the goal?

Reword your goal so that it is achievable:

_____

_____

_____

_____

Realistic/Reasonable /Results-based /Relevant

As you will have read in the previous section, your goal needs to be a stretch. You want to step outside your comfort zone, grow and flourish.

1. Realistic

You also need to make sure that you are **realistic**. If your goal is to walk on the moon, you know (even before you begin) that your chances of reaching that goal are slim to none. However, you should not let that stop you. It is more realistic if you are twelve when you set that goal, and you can work to increase your

129

chances of success through hard work. I met an 82-year-old man recently who dreams of going into space. All he needs is $4,000,000 and he can book a flight with Richard Branson. Never give up on your dreams. Similarly, if your goal is to win the lottery, you have to buy a ticket, because without one you will never succeed!

Several factors are involved in the realism of your goal. Your own ability is probably the biggest factor. When I was 17, one of my career goals was to be a rock star. However, I didn't play any instruments, couldn't sing that well, and didn't want to be

> *Poor:* To have an exhibition at the National Art Gallery
>
> *Better:* Take painting classes at the local community center this Spring

famous. My goal was totally unrealistic for me. Other factors to consider include the ability of the people around you and the suitability of your environment. One more consideration is that a goal that is realistic for someone else is not necessarily realistic for you. Don't let that stop your dreaming. Dreams are an essential part of goal setting because they help us develop courage, hope, inspiration and a reason to live. Ambition has no limits, and when you accomplish your dreams, you will believe that anything is possible.

Although your need to be practical is probably the most important aspect of your aim, you also need to tie your goals to your sense of self. You don't want to set a goal that goes against your moral and ethical standards. You also want your goal to be in line with your core values, and overall vision. In this way, you will be fully connected to your goal, and this will guarantee your success.

> If you haven't thought about what your core values are, there is more information at www.ruleyourworld.ca

2. Reasonable

When you set a goal, it must be **reasonable** for you. For example, if your goal is to write a book you might set a goal of writing a set number of words each day. Alternatively, you could decide that you will write for a set period of time each day. A professional writer might be able to write 2000 words a day, but

131

they don't do anything but write. If you are working full time this number may be entirely unreasonable. Also, you might not be able to write every day, so your daily total becomes unachievable. You might consider a weekly number to aim for. You also need to consider how much time you want to spend writing your book, and how big your book is going to be.

Years ago, a group of friends and I decided to write a book. It was supposed to be a straightforward romance, and we each planned to write 200-300 words at a time and share the writing. For my friends, writing 200-300 words was a chore, one that took hours of their time. For me it was reasonable, and I ended up doing all the writing.

> *"You have to be reasonable with yourself and not feel guilty when things aren't perfect"*
> Jaclyn Smith

Another aspect of reasonable goal setting is prioritizing. Try to have goals of varying levels of importance, so that you aren't always in a panic to complete. If you set performance goals they are often more reasonable than defined, results-based goals (see below). For example,

132

setting a goal of "running a 10 Km race" is more reasonable than "winning the 10 Km race". Reasonableness is really about improving your chances of success. My weight loss goal is reasonable, trying to get back down to my young and fit weight is not.

3. Results-based

Goals that are **results-based** are ones that focus on the outcome rather than the process. These types of goal are sometimes easier to set, but may also be harder to complete. Examples of results-based goals are "to have $5000 in my bank account", or "to lose ten pounds in weight." These goals don't specify how you plan to reach the target, and you can use many different processes to achieve success. Because there is no process built into the goal, you can approach the goal in many different ways. Without the guidance of a process, you might lose motivation sooner; you might also get off track. You might even find yourself spending more time deciding how you are going to accomplish the goal than time working on the goal.

However, this type of goal is very powerful. You are most likely to meet your goals if they are results-based. They are the easiest to measure and the most rewarding to accomplish. By having a tangible result at the conclusion of your journey, you will be much more motivated to succeed. You will also be motivated to continue working on achieving your goals, even if the going gets a little sticky.

4. Relevant

Your goals need to be **relevant** to you and your life. Your goals should *matter* and be part of your bigger plan. They should drive you forward, and improve your life. I talked about this in the meaningful section.

Just because a goal is specific, measurable, achievable and time-bound does not mean that  it is relevant. To set a goal of "making 50 cupcakes today" fits the S, M, A, and T categories, but is only relevant if you need 50 cupcakes in the next couple of days.

134

When you look at the relevance of your goal, revisit the reasons why you wanted to achieve your aim. Make sure that the purpose matches the reasons. A young lady I met, Mel, had a goal *"to obtain certification in child welfare."* She had a dream and wanted to make a difference in the lives of the children in her community. Mel was young, married with a small child, and working part time at the local supermarket. When she looked into how to become a child welfare worker, she discovered that she had to have a bachelor's degree in social work. There was no way Mel could do that due to financial and family restrictions, so she had to rethink. She discovered that she could get a certificate in early childhood education at the local community college. With that, Mel could work at a daycare, or in an after school program. The shorter course would give her the credentials she needed to complete her revised goal. By going back to her original motivation, Mel was able to modify her aim so that it became SMART.

Again, by being flexible, you can find other ways to achieve your purpose. Just like Jason the wannabe dentist turned accountant, there are many ways to get your flashy car. You just need to keep an eye on the real goal.

Exercise 12

Is your goal realistic and reasonable?

Is it results-oriented and relevant?

If it is, yay! If not, rework your wording:

_____

_____

_____

_____

_____

T

Timely/Time-bound/Time limited

By adding a time factor to your goal, you are effectively telling yourself that you will complete it. Without that time factor, your goal becomes never ending. "I am living in a penthouse apartment with a river view," may be a great goal, but without the added "by the end of 2020," you have no motivation to complete.

1. Timely

A **timely** goal is one that is directly relevant to your current situation. There may come a time when the goal is no longer relevant. This doesn't mean that the aim goes away forever;

139

you might just need to postpone it for a later date. You may find that the goal no longer fits with your life circumstances. For many years, my goal was to be tenured faculty at a research University. When I look back on that goal, I realise that it was an end-point more than a goal. It was the next step in my career path. It was not even a career path I had chosen. I had an opportunity to become junior faculty at one of the most prestigious medical schools in the US, but I chose my family over my career. I believed that a similar chance would come again. It took me a long time to realize, that opportunity would never come again for me. My time had passed, and I left science to pursue another career. I have no regrets at leaving a career I worked so hard to develop. I am who I am, and I am where I am today because of what went before.

> "To set achievable goals, include specific dates and times. Be flexible with your schedule – but be well-defined and explicit with your time frame."
> Emma Frost, PhD

140

2. Time-Bound

A **time-bound** goal is one that relates specifically to the moment or distinct period of your life. The Toastmasters organization provides multiple opportunities for people to learn leadership skills in a safe environment. Over several years, people had encouraged me to move up the leadership ladder. I had always declined, feeling that the time was not right. Then one day I woke up and realized that the time was now perfect. I announced my plan to run for office. I campaigned, won the election and spent three years learning and growing.

You may also find that you can still achieve your goal, but in a different way. By going back to the reasons you set that goal, you can discover another way to get there. A friend of mine, part of the Toastmasters organization, was on the leadership path, but his life intervened. He wasn't able to run for office when he felt ready. Because David wanted to develop his leadership skills, he looked elsewhere. He became part of another organization, joined the board, and he was able to develop his leadership skills in a different environment. He didn't let go of his goal; he changed his journey to success.

The time-bound nature of your objective will also play into the realistic and reasonable aspects of the SMART acronym.

3. Time limited

Creating a deadline is a crucial part of goal setting. It helps to provide focus as you track your progress. When you create the goal, decide when you *need* to accomplish it. Decide when you *want* to achieve your goal. If you want to improve your education, you

Poor: Lose 50 pounds.

Better: Lose 50 pounds by December 31st.

can take as much time as you have to complete courses, certifications, and diplomas. If you have an exam coming up soon, you have to study now. The **timeline** of your process will depend on several factors.

Creating a deadline also provides a sense of urgency for the goal. When I started writing this

142

book, I set myself the deadline of completing the first draft by January 31st. However, I didn't set a time limit for completing the edits. I puttered my way slowly through the edits with no sense of urgency. Until April, when I was at a car dealership, waiting for my car to be serviced. The lady at the table next to me asked what the book was I was working on. She expressed interest in buying my book, and I told her it would be available at the beginning of May. All of a sudden, I had a deadline and an increased sense of urgency.

Develop a way to track your progress. Use a table such as the one shown below. Keep it handy so that you can fill it in, so that you are reminded of the goals that you have set and the steps you need to take to succeed. The beautiful thing about creating a time-limited goal is you can write it down on your calendar, which will, in turn, keep it at the forefront of your mind.

Your Goal:				
Starting point:	Deadline			Completed
Stages:				

If your goal is part of a bigger objective, then deadlines and time limits become even more important. This is how you will prioritize your goals.

Exercise 13

Does your goal have a deadline?

If so, you are doing great! If not, rework your wording to include a timeline:

_____

_____

_____

_____

_____

Exciting/ Educational/ Evaluated

1. Exciting

Adding **excitement** to your goal enhances your enthusiasm for the task at hand. How can you add excitement? You add excitement by tapping into your emotions.

As you write your goal, ask yourself the following questions:

- Am I excited by this goal?
- Does the prospect of achieving it make me feel happy?
- If I don't achieve this goal will I be disappointed?

If you answer yes to all these questions, then you probably have a motivational objective.

If you answer no to any or all of these questions, then you need to ask yourself if this actually is a goal you want to achieve.

You can also add some fun to the process of reaching the goal. Especially if you expect that part of the process will be hard work or scary. By adding some fun, it will make the effort more attractive. Finding a way to make it more enjoyable isn't always easy. When I made my goal to lose weight and improve my fitness level a few years ago, I joined a gym and started to work out. I lost a few pounds, but just walking on a treadmill or the elliptical was so boring I began to lose motivation. One day I was watching an aerobics class through the glass wall, and wondered what it would be like to join in. I was excited by the prospect of joining the class because it looked like it could be a lot of fun.

> "There is nothing more beautiful than seeing a person being themselves. Imagine going through your day being unapologetically you."
> Steve Maraboli

Two days later, I joined the class and took up position at the back of the room. I tried to keep up with the music and follow the coaches as they shouted instructions to sashay, hop turn and grapevine with my left leg, right leg and don't forget your arms. At the end of the class, the instructor pulled me aside and said, "*it doesn't matter if you can't do it properly, it is more important that you keep moving.*" However, I was having fun, so I kept up with the classes, flailing my arms around wildly, mambo-cha-cha'ing in the wrong direction and Z-stepping into the walls, for about three months until they changed the schedule and I could no longer attend the classes.

I think I would have given up on my goal long before that if I had stuck to the boring elliptical and treadmill. Find a way to add some fun as you work hard on your goals.

2. Educational

We create goals because we want to improve our life. The good news is, any goal that includes an **educational** component is guaranteed to make a difference. The learning might involve getting a new qualification, or increasing your knowledge of something. Adding an educational component might be a difficult phase of the process. You might be planning to lose weight, and wonder what you can learn in that process. Or you plan to run a marathon, and can't imagine educating yourself through that process. The immediate learning objective may not be clear. However, when you think through your process, you may see where you will learn. When losing weight, you may discover new ways of preparing food, or new recipes. When training for a marathon, you may learn how to avoid injury, or how to run properly. You may learn how to prioritize and organize your days.

There are many things to learn, and many ways to improve your knowledge. You often find that you learn something new no matter what your goal, and how you achieve it. The process of planning for success and then following the timetable will change you for the better. Don't be afraid to learn new things, to take chances and to admit you don't know everything. It can be quite liberating.

3. Evaluated

Life changes continuously. As you progress towards the successful completion of your goal, you also change. **Evaluating** your goals is an important part of the process. You will need to evaluate forward momentum, changing perspectives, and relevance to ensure you meet your deadlines. If you don't include some form of evaluation in the plan, you might find that you aren't able to accomplish your goal because the goal posts have moved. If you have

"A truthful evaluation of yourself gives feedback for growth and success"
Brenda Johnson Padgitt

planned to spend more time with someone special, you will not be able to evaluate your progress if you do not track the time you spend together. By maintaining your method of measurement, you can evaluate your progress accurately.

You also need to assess whether your goal is still SMART. As your life changes, your needs and wants often do as well. The best way to assess your goal is to go back to the reason statement that you wrote at the beginning. John's goal was to buy a house because he wanted to move away from home and put down roots. He lived in his parent's basement as he worked to save up the down payment. Then John met someone with whom he wanted to spend the rest of his life. She already owned a house that she loved, and so did he. He evaluated his goal and realized that it was no longer relevant to his life.

It helps a lot if you evaluate your progress towards your goal. As you have created a measurable goal, you can easily see if you are improving. By using a tracking sheet, you can stay on top of the headway you are making. If you don't monitor the direction you are taking, you might end up in entirely the wrong place! When I was a teenager, I used to go hiking in the countryside with my friends. One day we set the goal of walking eight miles through the hills to the next destination, where we could enjoy a sumptuous feast. We had looked at the map before we started out and there were two routes we could take. One much easier than the other. As a group, we decided to take the easier route, which went round the bottom of a mountain. That day it was my turn to lead, and we set off at a reasonable pace. I was so confident that I knew which way to go I didn't keep the map handy.

To cut a long story short, I took a wrong turn, and we ended up climbing the mountain. We were rewarded with incredible views and a great feeling of accomplishment, but we were three hours late at our destination and missed the meal. If I had kept an eye on the map, we would have taken the right turn instead of the left at the fork in the path. Because I wasn't monitoring our progress, we went a long way off our planned route and didn't achieve our goal.

The evaluation process includes a review of your goal and the process you are following. By continuously reviewing your goals, you can ensure that they continue to guide you in the direction you want to go.

Exercise 14

Is your goal exciting?

Does it contain an educational component?

How will you evaluate your progress?

_____

_____

_____

_____

_____

R

Recorded/ Rewarding/ Re-evaluated/ Re-assessed

1. Recorded

Recording your progress as you work towards your goal, will help you see steady improvement. I am saving money and am plotting the dollar amounts on a graph. Watching the line reach towards my goal is a strong motivator when my willpower is weak. You will also be able to predict potential problems that might get in the way of success.

There are many ways to record your progress. Using a chart, calendar, or journal are some of the easiest ways. I will discuss

157

accountability later (see p.205). Being accountable is a great way to track your progress.

2. Rewarding

There are two ways to look at **rewarding** in relation to your goals. A rewarding goal is one that provides you with real satisfaction upon completion. Losing weight to fit into your wedding dress is rewarding. Saving enough money to buy a new car is rewarding when you drive your lipstick-red Cadillac off the lot. Graduating with your diploma is incredibly gratifying. By developing your goal around a rewarding outcome, you will add motivation, excitement, and triumph to your goal.

You can also use rewards to keep yourself on track. Just like dangling a carrot before a horse, providing rewards for yourself as you complete stages in your process will also help to maintain your motivation to succeed. The rewards that you choose have to be something that you are gifting yourself. If your goal is weight loss, you might reward yourself with new outfits, or jewelry, or even a steak dinner! But not every time you lose a pound. The reward needs to be something that you will be driven to achieve.

You also need to make sure that you don't move the goalposts on your incentive phases. If you set your first incentive at 10 pounds, don't  say *'nine is close enough.'* It is tempting but remember, you are cheating only yourself. If you need to save $50,000 to buy your custom Cadillac, and you say $40,000 is enough, you won't be able to afford the Caddy you want. You can buy a Caddy, but it will be a make-do for now Caddy (and we all know that when we make do, we are putting up with less than we deserve). By moving the goal posts, you change your destination.

There may be times when reaching that first stage has been tough. In this case, you might want to reward yourself and then change the process so that your stages aren't so difficult.

You don't want to become discouraged if progress is hard work!

I talked earlier about potentially changing direction if other aspects of your life change. This is sometimes unavoidable. It is important to remember that you are the person that will benefit the most from having goals and achieving them. Personal goals work on the honor system. If you cheat on your preset phases, you are only cheating yourself. It is also very easy to give up when things get difficult. This is a tough one, because if you are used to being in a rut, it is very easy to fall back into it. Plus, ruts can become very comfortable.

If you find yourself falling back into bad habits or cutting corners, go back to your original goal. Go back to the sentence about why you wanted to achieve this aim and remind yourself of your final destination. Look  back at the pictures you collected, and reimagine yourself owning those clothes, that car, that chair on the beach, or that job. Talk to your support network, ask for encouragement. That is what they are there for.

Just before I left the UK, I met up with a friend. She and I had been really close for many years. We both knew that when I left, we probably would never meet again because our lives were diverging. I can still remember her words to me "*I will be really mad at you if you mess this up.*" I knew that she was giving me her support, even though she was really sad that I was leaving for good.

If you are stuck, go to my website and sign up for one of the help packages.

3. Re-evaluating

Re-evaluating your goals is important. As I mentioned before, life is not a direct trajectory. You need to allow some wiggle room in your plan so that you can be flexible. If you are working to lose weight and are invited to three weddings in one month, you might want to move an intermediate deadline. This is part of being realistic. Unless you have incredible will-power, you may fall off the wagon from time to time. There is nothing wrong with this. It is called, "being human."

So instead of giving up when this happens, continue with your original goal and push your deadline back. By keeping one eye on your original motivation, you can always get back to where you were originally. Setbacks are just bumps in the road. They only become insurmountable if you let them.

Don't be discouraged. Remember Oprah Winfrey was fired from her position as co-anchor at a news channel because she was considered unfit for TV. J.K. Rowling had her Harry Potter manuscript rejected 12 times before someone finally gave her a chance. There are many other stories of how persistence has paid off. The important thing is not to give up.

You do not need to include this **R** in the wording of the goal. It should, however, be part of the process you have devised to ensure success.

Exercise 15

Does your goal fit the SMART criteria?

Your Goal:		
Specific	Is there enough detail for clarity?	
Measurable	How will you measure it?	
Action	How are you going to complete the goal?	
Relevance	Is it applicable to your growth?	
Time	Do you have a deadline?	

F for Flexible

Because goals have end-points, and life is not a direct trajectory through time, things change that might affect your long-term plans. Flexibility is crucial. Change doesn't mean that you have to give up on your goal. It might mean pushing your deadlines forward, or breaking your goals into smaller phases. But sometimes you have to accept that your journey isn't going to be a smooth one.

A colleague of mine told me that he had always wanted to propose to his girlfriend under a starry sky in the wilderness. He had set this goal when he was a young man before he even had a girlfriend. He had planned to take his current sweetheart to California and hike into Yosemite, pitch a tent and propose under a full moon. He had planned the whole thing, and she knew nothing about it. Two days before their vacation he fell

"Choose a summit; make a plan to reach there! If you think you can't make it, choose a new summit, make another plan. Or give up the summits, make new plans, find lower targets! In short, be 'flexible' in life!"
Mehmet Murat ildan

off a ladder and broke his heel. He had to have surgery, and so the trip was canceled. It was going to take a year for his foot to heal.

Three weeks later, they found out that they were going to be parents. Andy's goal of proposing under the stars in the wilderness had to change because he and his partner wanted their children to be born to married parents. He proposed to her by the reflecting pool at the Lincoln Memorial in Washington DC. It was wonderfully romantic, and she was thrilled.

They finally made it to Yosemite about five years later, with two children in tow, and stayed at the park hotel.

Part II

How to Ensure Success

How to Ensure Success

Imagine that you decide to go on vacation. You wouldn't just show up at the airport with your packed bags. You need to plan some things before you leave the house.

You need to decide where you want to go, when, and how you will get there. Also, you need to decide who will go with you, where you will stay and how long you will be away. You also need to decide what to pack! The more planning you put into your vacation, the more likely you are to have a fabulous time.

> "The journey of a thousand miles begins with one step."
> Lao Tzu

Making goals is much the same. The more planning you do, the more likely it is you will succeed.

When you write down your goals, think about the steps that you will need to ensure success. Much as with your vacation plan, you need to decide where and when you are "going" and how you will get there. In addition, who are the people you will take along with you who will help you succeed? Some of this will be written into the goal. The "where" the "how" and the "how long" are part of the SMART aspects.

Another crucial point to consider as you develop your goals is potential roadblocks. It isn't 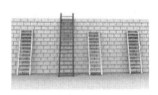 always possible to know if something will go wrong but in general assume that *if it can go wrong, it will go wrong.*

Another important fact is that no matter how much willpower you start with, it can run out. You use willpower to ignore distractions at work, control your temper when frustrated, and avoid a second helping of ice cream after a bad day at work. Each of us has a limited supply of self-control. The more you have to control one aspect of your life, the less willpower you will have available for other aspects of your life. Remember the last time you were in line at the supermarket checkout and the couple ahead of you were arguing for ten minutes over the price of every other item in their cart? Your drive home was much more frustrating because you had already used up a lot of self-control staying calm at the checkout.

There are ways to help you improve your willpower. Zenhabits.net suggests we practice self-control. They recommend pushing your mental energy until you are exhausted. Solving 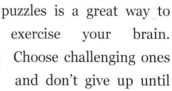 puzzles is a great way to exercise your brain. Choose challenging ones and don't give up until you have to. You can also practice self-control by deliberately putting yourself in a situation you would normally react to, and not react. For example, they suggest going shopping when you are famished. Resisting the urge to fill your cart with snacks is a great way to test your self-control.

Another way to improve your willpower is to plan ahead. If you can anticipate when you will need more willpower, you can avoid stress before your event. For example, if you know you are going to do your tax return on Saturday, don't plan on going shopping at Costco with your kids in the morning.

Meditation can also help re-energise your brain. As little as ten minutes a day can make a big difference in your self-control. You can also change your diet and exercise routine. Fresh fruit and vegetables are known to be beneficial for brain health. Many studies have shown that exercise can increase blood flow to the brain, relax you, and distract you from the stresses of the day. An added bonus is that it helps you lose weight! Then there is chocolate, which is a cure-all for most ills. Only you know how you can relax and refresh, just remember to schedule rest into your schedule.

By postponing an activity, you can also relieve yourself of some of the stress associated with avoiding it. By saying "not now but later," you remove some of the temptation to indulge now.

TROUBLESHOOTING

Troubleshooting is a form of problem solving. It is a skill that you can quickly learn. Most of the time we troubleshoot when things have stopped working. You have plateaued with your weight loss, you haven't been able to put any money aside for your vacation this month, or you just haven't had the time to read much lately. These are all reasons why your progress might have stalled.

However, one aspect of planning is working out what might go wrong, and having a plan B in place. It is like packing Pepto-Bismol when going away. You don't know that you will, but just in case you get a stomach upset while away from home, you have your friendly pink liquid on hand.

When something has gone wrong, we start troubleshooting by looking at the most obvious possible reasons for the failure. If you get the blue screen of death on your computer, you reboot. If that doesn't work, then you try booting into safe mode. The very first time your screen went blue, you probably panicked and got help from someone you trusted. The more times it happens, the faster you can fix the issue. If you had thought ahead when you bought the computer, you would have found out how to deal with a crash. Of course, we don't expect our equipment to fail, yet there are always possibilities.

> "A sum can be put right: but only by going back till you find the error and working it afresh from that point, never by simply going on."
> C.S. Lewis

One of the best ways to troubleshoot in advance is too look at the steps involved in your process and identify areas that might cause issues. This five-step process can help:

1. Verify that a problem may exist.
2. Identify the cause of the problem.

176

3. Work out how you can fix the cause of the problem.

4. Verify that your fix will correct the problem.

5. Assess to ensure the fix won't create another problem.

Step five in this process is necessary to prevent a quick fix creating more problems. I once took a road trip in an old car. A very old car. It broke down on the second day. Back then, I was quite good at maintaining my car, and so popped the hood  to see if I could fix it. The fan belt had broken causing the engine to overheat. I was miles from anywhere, on a deserted road, so I did what any other girl scout would do. I used a pair of pantyhose as a substitute belt. It worked very well. A little too well, because I forgot that it was only a temporary fix. Three weeks later, my car broke down again. This time, I couldn't fix it. Not only had the pantyhose belt fallen apart, but also the head gasket had blown. The entire engine had to be replaced. Fortunately, I was within walking distance of a garage. Unfortunately, my car was totaled. My quick fix turned out to be extremely expensive! A quick assessment of the fix would have highlighted the inevitable destruction of my car if I didn't find a permanent solution to the problem.

Troubleshooting is essentially a *"what if"* scenario. By asking yourself *"what will happen if this goes wrong?"* It isn't necessary to cover every eventuality because that will take the rest of your life. It is more important to recognize significant threats to your success.

> *"The emphasis on 'Plan B' that professionals talk about is not a coward's fall-back system. It serves a purpose, that a strategist has envisioned and planned before the need for an alternate solution surfaces."*
> Andy Paula

If your goal is to be promoted at work, one of the things that could go wrong is someone else getting the promotion ahead of you. How will you deal with that? There are at least two ways to overcome this barrier; one is to push

178

your deadline forward; the other is to find alternative employment that will give you the promotion you seek. By identifying this potential hurdle, you can plan ahead to increase your chances of success. In addition, proper preparation will increase your chances of success. You can also find out the company expectations, the skills you need to demonstrate to increase your chance, who else is vying for the job, and who is making the ultimate decision. The final question will make a big difference if that person is someone you dislike, or who dislikes you!

Planning in this way will markedly increase your chances of succeeding. Or it might make you reconsider the process that you have developed. The most important point to remember is not to give up! Nothing is insurmountable. There is a way around every hurdle. Your journey might take longer, and you might need to bring in more help, but the most important thing to remember is that you will get there in the end, as long as you don't give up. There is no shame in getting more help.

You can use this checklist as you work through your plan:

Checklist:

1. Why did I choose this goal?
2. What is the activity to be accomplished?
3. What do I need to do?
4. What do I need to have?
5. What do I need to learn?
6. What resources are available to me?
7. Whom can I ask for help?
8. Is this the best way of achieving this goal?
9. What are the potential obstacles that may get in the way of my access?
10. How can I avoid those barriers?
11. How much will reaching this goal cost? (Financial cost, resources, time)

Exercise 16

Write your SMART goal here:

_____

_____

_____

Whom will you take along with you?

_____

_____

_____

What do you need to take with you on your journey?

_____

_____

_____

_____

What do you need to do *before* you begin?

_____

_____

_____

Which are the stages where things might go wrong?

_____

_____

_____

_____

Can you prevent any of these issues?

How will you deal with them if they do go wrong?

_____

_____

Any other thoughts you have that will help you succeed.

BREAK YOUR GOALS DOWN

B reak each goal into smaller stages and plan how you will complete each phase. Each stage can become a goal on its own. If your primary objective is a long-term goal, you can break it down into intermediate-term, short-term and immediate goals.

If your goal is to climb Mount Everest, you do not just fly to Nepal and start climbing. Many things need to be put in place before you even get to the airport. Even when you get to Nepal, you cannot climb the mountain in one go. You have to break the climb into numerous stages. There are four camps, and five stages of the climb. You need to have climbing gear, guides, permits, and supplies. You have to raise money and get fit. You also have to be prepared to be away from home for over three months.

Unlike climbing Everest, it isn't always easy to break something down into phases. Think about your goal as you would your vacation, and decide what you need to do to get to your destination.

> "You do not climb a mountain like Everest by trying to race ahead on your own, or by competing with your comrades. You do it slowly and carefully, by unselfish teamwork. Certainly I wanted to reach the top by myself; it was the one thing that I had dreamed of all my life."
> Tenzing Norgay

If your goal is to read forty books before December 31st, you can break it down to one book every nine days. That will keep you on track. You could also write a list of the forty books that you want to read, and sort them. By sorting them into categories, it will make it easier to choose the next book you wish to read. Alternatively, if you sort them into the order that you want to read them, you will save time when you complete each book. It may be that you want to complete your list by reading a classic novel with a light, cozy mystery in

186

between. However you choose to break the list down, it will make the task seem less intimidating.

As you break down your goal into smaller steps, you can also create a calendar of success. You can either write them in a diary, with deadlines and warnings written in. Or you can create a schedule. There are many different calendar templates available online that you can use for this planning technique. A third way you can create a program is to take your goals, decide how long each will take, and then plot them on a grid (see below).

An advantage of this method is that it allows you to see if you are overloading yourself at any point in the year. In the example below, only two of the three goals overlap at any one time.

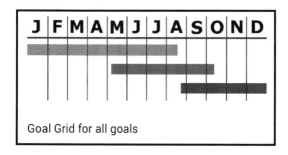

Goal Grid for all goals

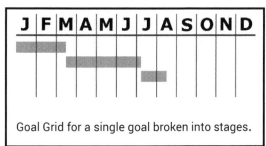

Goal Grid for a single goal broken into stages.

You can also break each goal into stages, and plot them on a similar grid. In this way, you can also see if you can break one of the phases down further. In this example, the second stage will take almost four months to complete. You might want to split it into two smaller steps to make it less overwhelming.

If you are looking at a long-term (three years or more) goal, plotting the stages on a grid will also help you to visualize the commitment you are making. You can also see where goals may overlap, and gaps appear as you wait for the perfect time to complete the goal.

Grid for Three Year Goal Plan

Exercise 17

Choose one of your goals:

_____

_____

_____

_____

Break it down into three to five steps. If you have more than five steps, break it into two goals:

1.
_____

2.
_____

3.
_____

4.
_____

5.
_____

You now have a series of steps to complete. How long do you think each one will take?

If you are going to be learning new skills, you may not be able to assess accurately how much time you need. This is another area of goal setting that requires some flexibility. It may require learning time-management skills. In reality, you can't manage time; you can only manage your activities in relation to time. However, this is a useful skill to develop, especially if you have a long to-do-list.

Goal:				
Step	Days	Weeks	Months	Years
1				
2				
3				
4				
5				

Note that if one step in the process takes longer than you had anticipated, you may have to change the whole timeline of the goal, perhaps even the final deadline.

Once you have broken the goal down into steps or phases, you can create deadlines for each step:

Goal:		
Step	Start date	End date
1		
2		
3		
4		
5		

Complete this exercise with each of your goals. You can download more worksheets on the website www.ruleyourworld.ca

Once you have created timelines and deadlines for your goals, create a calendar using the following template. Block off the time each objective will take. You can download a printable template from the website, which you can complete, print and keep for constant reference.

This exercise will show you how your goals and tasks overlap.

Goal	J	F	M	A	M	J	J	A	S	O	N	D

PRIORITIZE

If you have created a timeline for every goal and completed Exercise 16, you may have realized that some or all of your goals and tasks overlap. You may even have everything happening all in one month! Unless you are a superhero (like me), you will not be able to complete your goals without some seriously hard work. Hard work is no fun!

This book is designed to help you learn and grow. Therefore, it is imperative that you work out a complete schedule to minimize the hard work. The easier you make the process, the more likely you are to succeed. If we go back to Everest, the idea of climbing a mountain that

195

claims the lives of many adventurers every year seems like an impossible task. You don't even know how you would start to climb to the highest point on earth. So you read up on it. Then you realise that if you raise a minimum of $25,000, spend two years training, buy permits, hire guides, and book flights it could be possible. Once you have done all the research, read stories, consulted experts, planned how to raise the money, worked out a training schedule and discovered how to get permits and hire guides, your impossible dream becomes an achievable goal!

Part of the success-plan process is making sure that you complete your tasks in the best order possible. The easiest way to prioritize your goals is to write them down, and then reorder them according to the deadline you have assigned to them. Hopefully, not all your goals have the same December 31st deadline!

Sometimes the priorities will sort themselves out because you must achieve one goal to succeed with another. For example, you have two goals 1) "*Get promoted at work by December 31st*"; and 2) "*Improve my leadership skills by taking a training course offered by a private coach.*" To achieve 1, you need to complete 2. Therefore, the priority becomes 2 then 1. When baking a cake, you don't mix the eggs and milk into the flour before working in the butter. If you do, you will not get a cake at the end of the baking.

As mentioned before, you can create big goals that are made up of several (or many) smaller ones. If that is the case, you will need to complete the short-term goals in the best order to increase your chances of reaching the long-term objective. Sometimes it is obvious which order you need to complete the stages, sometimes it isn't.

> "The key is not to prioritize what's on your schedule, but to schedule your priorities."
> Stephen Covey

If there is no obvious way to prioritize your goals, then choose whichever order you wish. You may choose the harder ones first and finish with the easier aims. Or the easy ones first.

You can also work on more than one goal or task at a time. This might take a lot more organizing, and careful assessment of your timelines. It might also require you to be realistic about the amount of work that you can get done in a specified amount of time. It can take practice to know how long a task will take, so don't be discouraged if things take longer to do than you had hoped. As you learn how to better manage the tasks that you have to complete in the amount of time that you have, you will find that you get more and more done.

Exercise 18

Choose three of your goals and prioritize them:

1.
_____

2.
_____

3.
_____

In order of priority

1.

_____

2.

_____

3.

_____

With your newly prioritized list of goals, you can now replot your calendar.

Goal	J	F	M	A	M	J	J	A	S	O	N	D

REVIEW YOUR GOALS FREQUENTLY

You have come up with some appealing goals, written them down, and broken them down into smaller steps.

You have created a beautiful calendar to ensure that you stay on track and complete your goals before your self-imposed deadline. Now you need to remind yourself that you have goals for the year.

Reread your plan regularly.

Depending on the complexity of the goal, you may want to review your progress weekly, or, at least, monthly.

This helps you to remember your original vision, as well as to make the goals real. At the same time, you can assess whether the goal still meets the SMART criteria. Things change, nothing changes more than life, and you need to be flexible with your goals.

Another advantage of reviewing your goals through the year is that each time you review, you will remind yourself of your goal and what it is you wanted to achieve. In this way, you markedly increase your chances of success.

Don't forget to re-read the sentence you wrote explaining why you wanted to meet this goal.

"It's the possibility of having a dream come true that makes life interesting."
Paulo Coelho

BE ACCOUNTABLE

If you do not make yourself responsible for your own success, you can very quickly just "forget" about your goals.

There are a few easy steps that you can take to learn how to be accountable:

1. Be Responsible

Being responsible means that whether you succeed, or fail, you will own the outcome. Try not to think about "*shoulda, woulda, coulda,*" accept what IS, and react accordingly. Change what you need to, and move on. Most of all, learn from your mistake and *choose* not to repeat it.

> "Accountability breeds response-ability."
> Stephen Covey

205

2. Be Empowered

You are the only person who can empower you. You decide what you expect of yourself. You are the only person who can convince yourself that you really can do it. If you need to, write down all the things that you excel at. When self-doubt creeps up on you, read this list. Read it out loud (that makes it more real), and read it until you believe it. Learn how to say no, and stand by your word. Most importantly, don't let naysayers put you off aiming high with your goals. Part of empowerment is overcoming fear. Everyone is afraid of something. Unless it is a pathological phobia, you can overcome any fear with time and the right help.

3. Be Honest with Yourself

Everyone makes mistakes. When you do, accept them and learn from them. Don't try to cover up those errors, this will only add layers of stress. Don't be too hard on yourself when errors occur; it will only bring on more self-doubt. A good friend of mine asks herself if anyone died as a result of her mistake, and if the answer is

206

no, she lets it go. Be honest about your limitations, no one person can do everything. We all need help, and it is not a sign of weakness to ask. Realize that with your limitations comes the risk of failure, and remember that every winner has lost many more times than they have won.

Some people say that you should tell other people what your intentions are. The best people to share your goals with are people invested in helping you succeed. Such people include mentors, mastermind groups, or partners. If you don't have a local support group, join the group on the website (www.ruleyourworld.ca). You can share your objectives with the discussion group, and gain support and encouragement from others working on the book.

Also, be aware that there may be occasions when you don't want to share your goals. For example, if you are trying to get out from being under someone else's control, it might be beneficial to keep your goals quiet.

You may also want to keep your plans secret if you intend to surprise someone with your accomplishment at the end of the process. This would fit if your goal were to create a book about your family history to give to your grandmother on her 100th birthday.

Research on goal setting has shown that confidence in your ability to complete the task, success with previous goal achievements, and family/community influences will affect the way you set your goal. It isn't always easy to overcome these outside influences, and they may result in the need to keep your plans private.

> "You can do anything as long as you have the passion, the drive, the focus, and the support."
> Sabrina Bryan

On the other hand, you might want to share with someone you trust to help you overcome your doubts and lack of self-assurance. Most of the time we are more than capable of performing a task. The only thing stopping us is our self-doubts.

There are many support groups available for various activities that you may be participating in. Book clubs, running clubs, health support groups, will all be available in your community. If you can build a support group around you, the chances of your success are heightened further. This is why Weight Watchers works so well for so many people. The safe and encouraging environment in these groups may work well to help you succeed.

Exercise 19

How will you make yourself accountable for your success?

1.
_____

2.
_____

3.
_____

Exercise 20

Now that you know how to write goals, go back to your original list of things that you wanted to accomplish (p.29). Turn that list into achievable goals.

Try to complete at least five goals, of different types (health, self, family, financial, community) and in different categories (short, intermediate, long, life)

1.

_____

2.

_____

3.

_____

4.

_____

5.

_____

I would love to hear how you get on. Join in the
discussion on my website
www.ruleyourworld.ca

Good luck!

Part IV

The Final Word

THE FINAL WORD

When we are children, and real life does not limit our dreams, we set our goals high. We want to be astronauts, doctors, rock stars, pilots, or ballet dancers. As we age, we limit ourselves to careers that are considered realistic such as teaching, engineering, administration, accounting, or nursing. We need to be realistic about life. However, society forces us to fit in, and we have bills to pay, so we lower our expectations. Yet somewhere, deep down inside, there is still a tiny part of us that wants to dance Swan Lake, play guitar in front of a sell-out crowd, or walk on the moon.

Give that little part of you a voice. Live that dream. You might need to scale back on your goals, but that doesn't mean that you shouldn't dream big.

In the words of Winston Churchill, *"you should never, never, never give up."*

There are many inspiring stories about not giving up. One I heard recently was a mother of three children who wanted to run a marathon. She had run several marathons before she had married. During her pregnancies, she had put on a lot of weight, and had struggled to get back into shape. One day she was showing her son her marathon medals, and he asked why she had stopped running. She didn't know the answer to that, or to his question about why she hadn't started running again. She decided that she had to run one more marathon to prove to herself that she could. It took her two years to regain race fitness so  that she was allowed to run the full 26.2 miles. On race day, her family was lined up to watch her. At the start of the race, she felt strong and confident and was enjoying the run. By the tenth mile, she was beginning to wonder if she would beat her own personal best. Suddenly, at the fourteenth mile, she hit the wall. This was not a new experience for her, but never this early in the race. She focused on running just a few more yards, and then a few more. She kept moving forward. At the sixteenth mile, she stumbled and fell against the fence.

She leaned against the fence for a few minutes before staggering back out onto the course. She wasn't able to run, so she half-jogged half walked. She got slower and slower, but she was determined to get to the end. Finally, she could see the finish line ahead, but by then she was barely moving. She couldn't even hear the crowds yelling encouragement. She was focused on finishing and had only 500 meters to go when she put her foot down on a drink packet that had been discarded by another runner. Her ankle turned over as she fell. The pain shot up her leg, and she rolled over in agony. Her husband and son were

> "Many of life's failures are people who did not realize how close they were to success when they gave up."
> Thomas Edison

suddenly by her side, and she looked up at them. She said afterward that the look of disappointment on her 7-year-old son's face was enough to remotivate her. Something flashed through her brain saying that she couldn't disappoint him.

She tried to stand, but the pain in her ankle was so great that she fell back on the ground. Determined to finish, and cheered on by the large crowd, she started to crawl. When she crossed the finish line her hands and knees were bleeding, she felt sick, dizzy and her ankle had swollen to the size of a grapefruit. But the feeling of accomplishment overcame everything else, and she finished with a great big smile on her face. She could have stopped many times, given up on her dream to run one last marathon. However, she had to prove to herself that she could do it.

> *"Don't quit. Never give up trying to build the world you can see, even if others can't see it. Listen to your drum and your drum only. It's the one that makes the sweetest sound."*
> Simon Sinek

Chasing your goals is like running a marathon. You have to plan for success, train hard, and never give up until you reach the finish line no matter what happens along the way.

For most of us, we will not have to suffer great pain, or sacrifice as we pursue our goals. However, the commitment to success will be the same. The only way to succeed is not to give up. You might need to change your plans. You might need to revise your deadlines. You might need to add more steps in your process. But you should never give up on your dreams.

While you are planning to succeed, there are a few things you need to know. There are three types of people who will never prevail:

1. complainers,
2. people who tell everyone they are awesome, and
3. those who talk about other people behind their backs.

Complainers see the downside of life, and they bring themselves down, and they also bring the people around them down. It isn't always easy to switch from a pessimist to being an optimist. It takes time and hard work, but it is worthwhile in the end. Sometimes negative people don't even realise that they are downers. When someone pointed it out to me, I was truly shocked. From that time on, I tried to be more positive.

People who tell everyone how awesome they are become tedious. It is ok to boast from time to time, just not all the time. In truth, people who self-aggrandize are often not respected, and frequently not listened to. People will often avoid a bragger. It's hard to make friends when you're the most arrogant person in the room. Arrogant bosses are usually the most disliked of all bosses.

Those who indulge in gossip are commonly considered untrustworthy. They are looking to undermine someone by belittling them, or trying to turn other people's opinions against them. Again, there is a lot of negativity involved in gossip and a lot of unfairness, as the subject is not able to defend themselves against the defamation. Gossip is one of the most destructive forms of conversation. It destroys the speakers as well as the subjects.

Lack of Success

Another point that you need to remember is that you will fail. You will fail at least once, maybe many times. It is vital that you learn from each failure. These failures may take the form of a failed relationship, a failed career choice, an inability to predict a catastrophic event. The importance of failure is that each mistake you make is a different one. You can learn from each failure.

> "Our greatest glory is not in never falling, but in rising every time we fall."
> Confucius

When things go wrong, look back at the troubleshooting techniques described above (p.175), and work your way back to the right path. You also need to ensure that you are failing at the right things. That means not making the same mistakes over and over again. It also means that your failures are learning opportunities so that next time you are better prepared.

You now have the tools you need to create fabulous goals for yourself. You know how to work them, how to set deadlines, create a success plan, and most importantly, you have decided to grow.

All you have to do now is get started! Nothing is stopping you from being the best person you can be.

So:

- Stop making excuses.
- Take risks.
- Stretch yourself.
- Think outside the box.
- Be consistent.
- Be responsible.

And most of all,

Be Fabulous!

Download the worksheets at

www.ruleyourworld.ca

"The Quick and Easy Way to Take Control of Your Life - What the internet won't tell you about goal setting."

A program run by CanLead Training.

~ Emma Frost ~

THE PEOPLE

BEHIND

THE QUOTES

THE PEOPLE BEHIND THE QUOTES

Jim Rohn (1930 – 2009) was one of the most influential motivational speaker/trainers in the field of personal development. He inspired people to expand their perspective of success and change their lives for the better. (p.s 13, 25, 99)

Max De Pree is an American businessman and writer. He encouraged and rewarded employee participation. Max is a student of human nature and life, and the author of several books including *Leadership is an Art, Leading without power and Called to Serve.* (p.21)

Deborah Day, author of several books including *Be Happy Now* and creator of the Women's Twelve Week Empowerment Group. She was a clinician in the mental health field for more than twenty-six years. (p.37)

Richard Nelson Bolles is a former Episcopal clergyman and author of the best-selling job-hunting book; *What Color is Your Parachute? - A practical manual for job hunters and career-changers.* (p.41)

Deanna Ford is an author, speaker, filmmaker, and eco-optimist. A military musician turned environmental advocate; she is very active in her local environmental community. Her book *The Eco-Optimist's Guide to Saving Our Planet* will be available in the Fall of 2016. (p.45)

Dr. Steve Maraboli is a professional speaker, bestselling author, and behavioral scientist specializing in leadership dynamics, and the Peak Performance Mindset. (p.s 52 & 148)

Jack Canfield is a motivational speaker and trainer. He co-authored *Chicken Soup for the Soul* and wrote several other books including

The Success Principles, The Power of Focus and Maximum Confidence: Ten Secrets of Extreme Self-Esteem. Jack is the founder of the Transformational Leadership Council. (p.s 54 & 125)

Ralph Waldo Emerson was an American essayist, lecturer, and poet who led the Transcendentalist movement of the mid-19th century. (p.62)

Lorii Myers is a Canadian entrepreneur with senior management experience, she is a business owner, and award-winning author of the *3-Off the Tee* series. With the belief that the right attitude is everything, she believes you should aspire to learn from those who inspire you. (p.78)

Alan Alda is an award-winning actor, director, screenwriter, and author. He is best known for his roles as Hawkeye in M*A*S*H and Arnold Vinick in The West Wing. (p.79)

Emily Levine is an American humorist, writer and public speaker who lectures on the meaning of life from a scientist's point of view. (p.81)

Debbie Ford (1955-2013) was an internationally recognized expert in the field of personal transformation she wrote three books including *The Secret of the Shadow*. Her books are groundbreaking works in emotional and spiritual education. (p.88)

Evelyn Mary Dunbar (1906-1960) was a British artist and a forerunner of the Green movement. She was known as one of the few female artists employed by the War Artists' Advisory Committee to record women's contributions to World War II on the UK home front. (p.102)

Jenny Craig is an American weight-management and nutrition guru who in 1983, founded Jenny Craig Inc. (p.105)

Edward de Bono is a physician, psychologist, author, inventor and consultant. He originated the term "lateral thinking," and authored several books, including *Six Thinking Hats, How to be More Interesting*, and *Teach Yourself to Think*. (p.122)

Gail Sheehy is a journalist, lecturer and award-winning author of seventeen books.

232

Gail's philosophies help women and men accept their life changes as they age. (p.123)

Jaclyn Smith is an American actor and businesswoman. She is best known as Kelly Garrett, one of Charlie's Angels, and is an inspirational businesswoman who began the trend of celebrities developing their own fashion brand. (p.132)

Brenda Johnson Padgitt is an author, radio host, speaker and an experienced educator. She has written several books, including *Articles for Personal Growth and Development: Volume I*, and *How Did I Get Into This Mess?* (p.151)

Mehmet Murat İldan is a contemporary Turkish novelist and award-winning playwright. (p.165)

Lao Tzu, an ancient Chinese philosopher, and writer, was the author of the Tao Te Ching and the founder of Taoism. (p.169)

C.S. Lewis (1898 – 1963) was a British novelist, scholar, and broadcaster. He is most well known for his Chronicles of Narnia books. (p.176)

Andy Paula is a corporate trainer, and a writer. She focuses on Soft Skills/ Behavioral Training, Presentations Skills, Public Speaking, and Team Building. Her books include *Soft Skills Mantras, Joba's Journey* and *Where Everywoman Leads*. (p.178)

Tenzing Norgay (1914 – 1986) was one of the most famous mountain climbers in history. He and Sir Edmund Hillary were the first two individuals known to reach the summit of Mount Everest. (p.186)

Stephen Covey (1932-2012) was an educator, author, and motivational speaker. He is most well known for his book *The Seven Habits of Highly Effective People*, which has sold more than 25 million copies worldwide. (p.s 197 & p.205)

Sabrina Bryan is an American singer, actor, author, songwriter, fashion designer, choreographer, dancer, and television personality best known as a member of the girl group The Cheetah Girls. (p.208)

Simon O. Sinek is a British author, speaker, and consultant. His books on leadership and management include *Start With Why: How Great Leaders Inspire Everyone to Take Action*, and *Leaders Eat Last: Why Some Teams Pull Together and Others Don't.* (p.220)

Paulo Coelho is a Brazilian lyricist and award-winning novelist. His books include *The Alchemist, The Valkyries*, and *By the River Piedra, I Sat Down and Wept.* (p.204)

Thomas Edison (1847 – 1931) was an American inventor and businessman. He developed many devices including the phonograph, the motion picture camera, and the long-lasting, practical electric light bulb. (p.219)

IMAGE CREDITS

All images created by the author (Emma Frost) or the following sources:

p.14 Image courtesy of "digitalart" at FreeDigitalPhotos.net

p. 24 Image available on "WikiCommons"

p.35 Image courtesy of "Heavypong" at FreeDigitalPhotos.net

p.51 Image courtesy of "Vectorilie" at FreeDigitalPhotos.net

p.67 Image courtesy of "Iamnee" at FreeDigitalPhotos.net

p.119 Image courtesy of "Mister GC" at FreeDigitalPhotos.net p.177 Image courtesy of "franky242" at FreeDigitalPhotos.net

p.s 153 & 195 Image courtesy of "Melscapit" on Fiverr

p.s 159, 160 & 170 Image courtesy of "Stuart Miles" at FreeDigitalPhotos.net

INDEX

INDEX

ABOUT THE AUTHOR

Emma is a Success Coach and Professional Speaker. She has been coaching and mentoring people since 2003. She is passionate about helping others to achieve their goals. Emma has spoken on personal growth, leadership skills and team development, as well as the benefits of evaluation, and motivation, for large and small groups. In her signature keynote address "Get out of your rut and get on with your life" Emma shares ideas on how to take back control of your life.

In 2008, Emma was a semi-finalist in the World Championship of Public Speaking (Toastmasters International), placing her in the top 85 speakers globally. Emma served as the Toastmasters International Governor for District 64 in 2012-2013. The organization is a world leader in communication and leadership development.

Since 2012, Emma has devoted herself to help people take control of their lives through personal growth. She was awarded her Ph.D. in Developmental Neuroscience in 1999 and worked at the US Navy Medical School and Johns Hopkins Medical School before moving to Canada.

Emma currently lives in Manitoba, Canada with her partner and their chihuahua, Spike.

Contact Emma at info@canlead.ca

CanLead Training

Founded in 2013, CanLead Training offers a customized experiential learning environment in which individuals identify their leadership skills and discover how to develop a plan to overcome obstacles to success. CanLead Training is known for their unique approach to coaching, and their ability to connect with each learner. This ensures that attendees know they have learned something new and leave ready to implement their personal growth plan.

By focusing on identifying and developing people's leadership skills, we help people think better, work better, live better, and Rule Their World!

For more information about Emma and the programs she offers see www.canlead.ca

Made in the USA
Charleston, SC
14 October 2016